Civil Procedure in Portugal

Civil Procedure in Portugal

Alexandre Dias Pereira

This book was originally published as a monograph in the International Encyclopaedia of Laws/Civil Procedure.

Founding Editor: Roger Blanpain
General Editor: Frank Hendrickx
Volume Editor: Wannes Vandenbussche

Wolters Kluwer

Published by:
Kluwer Law International B.V.
PO Box 316
2400 AH Alphen aan den Rijn
The Netherlands
E-mail: lrs-sales@wolterskluwer.com
Website: www.wolterskluwer.com/en/solutions/kluwerlawinternational

Sold and distributed by:
Wolters Kluwer Legal & Regulatory U.S.
920 Links Avenue
Landisville, PA 17538
United States of America
E-mail: customer.service@wolterskluwer.com

ISBN 978-94-035-2268-5

e-Book: ISBN 978-94-035-2278-4
web-PDF: ISBN 978-94-035-2288-3

This title is available on www.kluwerlawonline.com

The Author

Alexandre Dias Pereira is an Associate Professor at the Faculty of Law of the University of Coimbra, from which he received his Bachelor, Master and PhD in Law. He was an Erasmus Student of European and International Law at the Leuven Catholic University. He also teaches at Coimbra Business School and several postgraduate courses in Portuguese speaking countries, and lectures at national and international academic events, including the Salzburg Summer School on European Private Law. A former Director of Coimbra University Press, Alexandre Dias Pereira is a researcher at the Coimbra Institute for Legal Research ('Instituto Jurídico'), and a member of several scientific societies and editorial boards, having published several monographs as well as more than one hundred book chapters and review articles in Portuguese and international publications.

https://orcid.org/0000-0003-4356-9195

Email: aldp@fd.uc.pt

Table of Contents

List of Abbreviations

CC	Civil Code
CJEU	Court of Justice of the European Union
CPC	Civil Procedure Code [Código de Processo Civil]
CPLP	Community of Portuguese Language Countries
CRP	Constituição da República Portuguesa
DL	Decreto-Lei [Decree-Law]
EConHR	European Convention on Human Rights
EU	European Union
LOSJ	Lei da Organização do Sistema Judiciário
STJ	Supremo Tribunal de Justiça [Supreme Court of Justice]
TC	Tribunal Constitucional [Constitutional Court]
TRC	Tribunal da Relação de Coimbra [Coimbra Court of Appeals]
TRE	Tribunal da Relação de Évora [Évora Court of Appeals]
TRG	Tribunal da Relação de Guimarães [Guimarães Court of Appeals]
TRL	Tribunal da Relação de Lisboa [Lisbon Court of Appeals]
TRP	Tribunal da Relação do Porto [Oporto Court of Appeals]

Journals and Reviews

BFDUC	Boletim da Faculdade de Direito da Universidade de Coimbra
BMJ	Boletim do Ministério da Justiça
CDP	Cadernos de Direito Privado
CJ	Coletânea de Jurisprudência
RFDUL	Revista da Faculdade de Direito da Universidade de Lisboa
RLJ	Revista de Legislação e de Jurisprudência
ROA	Revista da Ordem dos Advogados

List of Abbreviations

Preface

This monograph aims to provide a comprehensive overview of the fundamental principles and key aspects of civil procedure in Portugal. Whether the reader is a law student, legal practitioner, or simply someone interested in understanding the mechanisms of justice in Portugal, this book will be a useful guide to learn more about Portuguese civil procedure law.

Civil procedure plays a crucial role in any legal system, as it sets the rules and procedures for resolving civil disputes between individuals, corporations, or other entities. In Portugal, like many other countries, an efficient and fair civil procedure is essential to ensure justice is served and the rights of all parties are protected.

This book offers a comprehensive resource that simplifies the complexities of civil procedure in Portugal and presents it in an accessible manner. To achieve this goal, the monograph is organized into several chapters, each focusing on a specific aspect of civil procedure. It starts with the historical evolution of civil procedure in Portugal, and then it delves into the basic principles of civil procedure, including the principles of access to justice, due process, and the right to a fair trial.

Throughout the book, the different stages of civil proceedings are explored, from the initiation of a lawsuit to the enforcement of judgments. Special attention will be given to the rules governing evidence, as well as the role of judges, attorneys, and other key actors in the civil litigation process.

Law is ever-evolving, and new developments may arise after the publication of this monograph. Therefore, readers are invited to explore further resources and to stay current with any changes in this field of law. The author hopes this book can be both informative and enjoyable, as well as a useful tool to understand Portuguese civil procedure law.

Coimbra, September 2023

General Introduction

§1. General Background (Geography, Demography, History, Political and Legal System)

1. Portugal is located in Southwestern Europe, on the Iberian Peninsula, with an area of 92,010 km^2 and a population of about 10.5 million people. Bordered by the Atlantic Ocean to the west and south and by Spain to the north and east, the territory of Portugal also includes the Atlantic archipelagos of Azores and Madeira. With Lisbon serving as its capital, the name of the country derives from Latin Portus and Celtic Cale. With traces of ancient Phoenician and Greek civilizations, the roots of Portugal are found in Lusitania, a Roman province of Hispania, later replaced by Germanic and then Islamic rule. Founded during the 'Reconquista' of the Iberian Peninsula, Portugal was officially recognized in 1143 as an independent State from León. Its first King was D. Afonso Henriques, who lies in Coimbra with his son D. Sancho I at the Monastery of Santa Cruz. Later on, the Portuguese navigators had a pioneer role in finding and exploring sea routes and expanding Christianity and European culture to other continents, mainly within the southern hemisphere and 'giving new worlds to the World'. Portuguese is one of the most spoken languages in the world, with more than 250 million speakers, most of them from Brazil.

2. On 1 January 1986, Portugal became a Member State of the European Communities and has been part of the EU and the Eurozone since the beginning. Portugal is also a member of the United Nations, OECD, NATO, WTO, the Schengen Area and CPLP. Portugal is among the twenty most visited countries in the world, receiving an average of 22 million tourists in 2022, and has a GDP of over EUR 250 billion. On 26 March 1995, Portugal started to implement Schengen Area rules, eliminating border controls with other Schengen members while simultaneously strengthening border controls with non-Member States. Expo 1998 took place in Portugal, and in 1999, it was one of the founding countries of the Euro and the Eurozone. On 1 December 2009, the Treaty of Lisbon entered into force, aiming to enhance the efficiency and democratic legitimacy of the Union and to improve the coherence of its actions.

3. Legal studies in Portugal date back to the foundation of the University during the reign of King D. Dinis, between 1288 and 1290. For centuries, the legal system of Portugal combined medieval local customary law and Roman law, derived from the ‘Corpus Iuris Civilis’. However, with the emergence of centralized power, unitary compilations have been adopted, notably the so-called Ordinations (Ordenações Afonsinas XV, Ordenações Manuelinas XVI and, under the Spanish King’s rule, Ordenações Filipinas XVII).

4. Portugal is a civil law country or continental legal system derived from Roman law. The main laws include the Constitution (1976), the Civil Code (CC) (1966) and the Penal Code (1982). Other relevant statutes in the field of Private law are, for example, the Commercial Code (1888), the Labour Code (2009), and the new Code of Civil Procedure (2013). The codification movement emerged in Portugal throughout the nineteenth century. The first CC entered into force in 1867 and is usually referred to as the ‘Código de Seabra’ after the name of its main drafter, Viscount of Seabra. The second and still in force CC was adopted in 1966.[1] The CC remains in force in some African Portuguese-speaking countries, notably Angola and Mozambique, and has served as a model for the codification in other Portuguese-speaking parts of the world, notably Macau (China) and East Timor. Notwithstanding, Portuguese codification started with commercial law. The first commercial code was enacted in 1837. Later on, Viscount Seabra was assigned the task of preparing the CC of 1867, which was in line with the liberal spirit of the time and received great influence from the French Civil Code of 1804 and from jus-rationalistic legal thinking. With the establishment of the Republic in 1910, the Code of Seabra was considerably amended.

5. The Portuguese political and legal system is based on a democratic framework established by the Portuguese Constitution of 1976.[2] The Portuguese Constitution serves as the supreme law of the country, providing the fundamental principles and rights of the citizens. It establishes the structure of the government, outlines the powers and responsibilities of each branch, and guarantees fundamental rights and freedoms. In fact, the Portuguese Constitution guarantees fundamental rights and freedoms to all individuals, including the right to life, liberty, and security, freedom of expression, assembly, and religion, and equality before the law. These rights are protected and enforced by the courts.

6. Portugal became a Republic in 1910. The 1976 Constitution of the Portuguese Republic, adopted after the April Revolution of 1974, provides that the Portuguese Republic is a sovereign Republic based on the dignity of the human person and on the will of the people[3] and a democratic State based on the rule of law, the sovereignty of the people, the pluralism of democratic expression and democratic political organization, respect for basic rights and freedoms and the separation and

1. Enacted by Decree-Law No. 47344 of 25 Nov. 1966, as last amended by Law No. 3/2023 of 16 January. Available at https://diariodarepublica.pt/dr/legislacao-consolidada/decreto-lei/1966-34509075.
2. Enacted by Decree No. 10/04 of 1976, as last amended by Law No. 1/2005 of 12 August. Available at https://diariodarepublica.pt/dr/legislacao-consolidada/decreto-aprovacao-constituicao/1976-34520775.
3. Article 1 of the Constitution.

inter-dependence of powers.[4] The validity of Statutes, regulations and other acts of public bodies requires conformity with the Constitution,[5] which is the main statutory source of Law.

7. The main components of the Portuguese political and legal system are the following. Powers of sovereignty are allocated to several bodies (órgãos), notably the President of the Republic, the Parliament or the Assembly of the Republic, the Government and the Courts.[6] The form of Government is a democratic republic, and the head of State is the President of the Republic, the highest office in the country, elected by popular vote to a five-year term.[7] He is also Commander-in-Chief of the Armed Forces. Presidential powers include the appointment of the Prime Minister and Council of Ministers; dismissing the Prime Minister; dissolving the Assembly; vetoing legislation; and declaring State of War or siege. The President is advised on issues of importance by the Council of State, which is composed of six senior civilian officers, any former Presidents elected under the 1976 Constitution, five members chosen by the Assembly, and five selected by the president.

8. The Executive Branch is headed by the Prime Minister, who is appointed by the President and approved by the Parliament. The government is responsible for the day-to-day administration of the country. The Legislative branch is the Parliament, known as the Assembly of the Republic, a unicameral legislature consisting of 230 members elected through a proportional representation system. The Parliament is responsible for making laws and overseeing the government's activities. As for the judicial branch, the judiciary is independent and separate from the executive and legislative branches. It ensures the application of the law, resolves disputes, and upholds individual rights.

9. The Legal System of Portugal is a Civil Law legal system, which is based on codified laws and statutes. The judicial system consists of various courts, including the TC, the Supreme Court of Justice (STJ) ('Supremo Tribunal de Justiça'), Courts of Appeal ('Relação'), Courts of First Instance ('Comarca'), the Administrative and Tax Courts, and other courts. The courts have jurisdiction over civil, criminal, administrative, and constitutional matters. The legal profession is carried out by Lawyers, known as 'Advogados'. They play a crucial role in the legal system, representing clients in legal proceedings and providing legal advice.

10. As for European Union (EU) Membership, Portugal has been a member of the EU since 1986. EU law has a significant impact on the Portuguese legal system, and EU regulations and directives are incorporated into national law.

4. Article 2 of the Constitution.
5. Article 3 of the Constitution.
6. Article 110 of the Constitution.
7. Article 128(1) of the Constitution.

§2. DELIMITATION OF THE SUBJECT MATTER

I. Definition of the Term 'Civil Procedure' ('Processo Civil')

11. Civil procedure, known as 'processo civil' in Portuguese, refers to the set of rules and procedures that govern the resolution of civil disputes between private parties. It specifically pertains to the judicial process for addressing civil claims and enforcing civil rights.

12. Civil procedure encompasses the legal framework and rules that regulate the proceedings, actions, and remedies available in civil matters. It covers a broad range of civil disputes, including contract disputes, tort claims, family law matters, property disputes, and more. Civil procedure is governed by the Civil Procedure Code (CPC).[8]

II. Distinction from Other Types of Procedure

13. Civil procedure is distinct from other types of procedure, such as administrative procedure and criminal procedure.

14. Administrative procedure pertains to legal proceedings concerning administrative matters, such as disputes with government agencies or challenges to administrative decisions. It operates under separate rules provided for by the Administrative Procedure Code.[9]

15. Criminal procedure governs the legal process for prosecuting and adjudicating criminal offences. It deals with criminal law violations and the prosecution of individuals accused of committing crimes. Criminal procedure operates under separate rules provided by the Criminal Procedure Code.[10]

III. Separate Court Systems and Rules of Procedure

16. Portugal has separate court systems for different types of cases, including civil, administrative, and criminal courts. Each court system has its own set of rules and procedures tailored to the specific type of case it handles.

---

8. 'Código de Processo Civil', enacted by Law No. 41/2013 of 26 June (revoked and replaced the previous Code of Civil Procedure, enacted by Decree-Law No. 44 129 of 28 Dec. 1961, and other special legislation on civil procedure).
9. 'Código de Procedimento Administrativo', enacted by Decree-Law No. 4/2015 of 7 January (replaced Decree-Law No. 442/91 of 15 November), as amended by Decree-Law No. 11/2023, of 10 February, and Law No. 72/2020 of 16 November.
10. 'Código de Processo Penal', enacted by Decree-Law No. 78/87 of 17 February (revokes and replaces Decree-Law No. 16489 of 15 Feb. 1929).

17. Civil cases are typically heard in civil courts, where the Code of Civil Procedure governs the proceedings, rules of evidence, and remedies available. Moreover, specific rules and procedures may apply to different types of civil cases, such as commercial disputes, labour disputes, or family law matters. For example, labour proceedings are heard before court divisions with specialized jurisdiction on labour matters and labour proceedings terms are set by the Code of Labour Procedure.[11] Insolvency proceedings are also dealt with by court divisions with specialized jurisdiction on insolvency matters (so-called 'juízos de comércio') where they exist[12] and under specific provisions provided by the Insolvency Code.[13]

§3. SOURCES OF CIVIL PROCEDURE LAW (INCLUDING A BRIEF HISTORICAL PERSPECTIVE)

18. The sources of Portuguese civil procedure law include legislation, codes, legal doctrine, and case law. Here is a brief overview of the historical perspective and key sources.

19. Legislation is the primary source of Portuguese law. Civil procedure law is governed by the Code of Civil Procedure ('Código de Processo Civil'), which sets out the rules and procedures governing civil litigation. Enacted in 2013,[14] the present Code replaced the previous code, which has been in force since 1961, and it is periodically updated to adapt to legal developments and changes in societal needs. As of January 2023, the Code had been amended thirteen times.[15]

20. Legal doctrine refers to scholarly writings and interpretations by legal experts, scholars, and academics. It plays a significant role in shaping and interpreting civil procedure law in Portugal. Legal scholars and experts provide commentary, opinion, analysis, and interpretation of the provisions of the CPC, helping to shape its application and understanding.

21. Concerning case law, judicial decisions by higher courts, particularly the STJ ('Supremo Tribunal de Justiça'), contribute to the development of civil procedure law in Portugal. Court decisions provide guidance on the interpretation and application of the law in specific cases, establishing legal principles and, to some extent, setting 'precedents', in particular the so-called judgments of jurisprudence standardization (acórdãos de uniformização de jurisprudência).[16]

---

11. 'Código de Processo do Trabalho', enacted by Decree-Law No. 480/99 of 9 November.
12. Articles 81(3)(i) and 128(1)(a) of LOSJ – 'Lei da Organização do Sistema Judiciário' (Judicial System Organization Statute), enacted by Law No. 62/2013 of 26 August (several times amended).
13. Enacted by Decree-Law No. 53/2004 of 18 March ('Código da Insolvência e da Recuperação de Empresas'), as last amended by Decree-Law No. 57/2022 of 25 August.
14. Law No. 41/2013 of 26 June, as last amended by Law No. 3/2023 of 16 January.
15. Available at https://diariodarepublica.pt/dr/detalhe/lei/41-2013-497406.
16. Case law available at http://www.dgsi.pt/.

22. From a historical perspective, Portuguese civil procedure law has evolved over time through various legal reforms and historical changes. The first comprehensive CPC in Portugal, known as 'Código de Processo Civil', was enacted in 1939 by Decree-law No. 29637 of 28 May,[17] replacing a fragmented and outdated procedural system. It marked a significant milestone in the organization and regulation of civil proceedings in Portugal. The code established a comprehensive set of rules and procedures to govern civil litigation and the resolution of civil disputes.

23. The development of the first Portuguese CPC was influenced by legal reforms taking place across Europe, particularly the wave of codifications in civil procedure during the nineteenth and early twentieth centuries. The code aimed to modernize and streamline civil litigation, providing a systematic framework for the conduct of civil cases in Portuguese courts.

24. The first CPC underwent subsequent revisions and amendments over the years to adapt to legal developments and changes in societal needs. It has been replaced by the codification of 1961, enacted by Decree-Law No. 44129 of 28 December, which introduced significant updates and reforms to align with modern legal principles and practices.

25. Subsequent reforms and amendments were made to adapt to legal developments, including the integration of EU law and the harmonization of procedural rules within the EU framework.

26. The most recent major reform took place in 2013, with the enactment of the current CPC, which aimed to streamline and modernize civil litigation in Portugal. The CPC is the crucial legal document that shapes the procedural aspects of civil litigation in Portugal. It sets out the rules governing the filing of lawsuits, court procedures, evidence, appeals, enforcement of judgments, and other important aspects of civil proceedings. Legal professionals, including judges, lawyers, and parties involved in civil cases, rely on the CPC as a primary source of procedural rules and guidance. Legal professionals, including judges, lawyers, and scholars, play a significant role in interpreting and applying the law.

27. Portuguese civil procedure law is subject to updates and modifications over time. In a decade after adoption, it has been amended more than a dozen times.

§4. General Features of the Administration of Justice in Civil Matters

I. Characteristics of the Procedure

28. In Portugal, the administration of justice in civil matters exhibits the following general features in terms of adversary/inquisitorial procedure, the role of the judge and parties, and oral and written aspects.

17. Available at https://files.dre.pt/1s/1939/05/12300/04190548.pdf.

29. In general, Portuguese civil procedure is an adversarial procedure with inquisitorial elements. It means that the Portuguese civil procedure is primarily based on an adversarial system, where the parties actively participate in presenting their arguments, evidence, and legal positions. They have the opportunity to assert their claims, counterclaims, and defences.

30. Notwithstanding, while primarily adversarial, there are also inquisitorial elements in Portuguese civil procedure. The judge takes an active role in managing the proceedings, ensuring procedural fairness, and seeking the truth by actively investigating and questioning the evidence presented.

31. Concerning the role of the judge and the parties, the judge in Portuguese civil proceedings has an active role in overseeing the proceedings, ensuring the proper application of the law, and making impartial decisions based on the evidence and arguments presented by the parties. The judge may also guide the parties and take measures to clarify or complete the facts and evidence. The parties have the responsibility to present their case, submit relevant evidence, and argue their positions. They actively participate in the proceedings, presenting their arguments and challenging the opposing party's claims. They have the opportunity to present witnesses, experts, and other evidence to support their case.

32. Moreover, Portuguese civil procedure includes oral hearings and discussions where parties present their arguments, examine witnesses, and make their case before the judge. Written submissions, including pleadings, motions, and briefs, also play a significant role in Portuguese civil procedure. Parties submit written documents containing their legal arguments, factual allegations, and evidence.

33. Other key features of civil procedure in Portugal include, for example, court-connected mediation and legal representation. On the one hand, Portuguese civil procedure encourages court-connected mediation as a means of alternative dispute resolution. Parties may be directed or voluntarily choose to participate in mediation to resolve their disputes with the assistance of a mediator. On the other hand, parties have the right to legal representation in civil matters, and lawyers play a crucial role in advocating for their clients' interests, preparing legal arguments, and navigating the procedural aspects of the case.

II. Fundamental Guarantees

34. The administration of justice in civil matters in Portugal is guided by fundamental guarantees, which are derived from various sources such as the Portuguese Constitution, international human rights treaties, and general principles of law. These guarantees ensure the protection of individuals' rights and the proper functioning of the civil justice system.

35. The Portuguese Constitution, as the supreme law of the country, provides a solid foundation for fundamental rights and principles in civil matters. It guarantees the right to a fair trial, access to justice, and due process. According to the STJ, 'The realization of justice must be achieved within the framework of the structuring principles of civil procedure, such as the principles of claim and contradictory, equality of the parties and impartiality of the judge, the main pillars of the fundamental principle of the equitable process proclaimed in Article 20 (4) of the Constitution.'[18]

36. First, everyone is guaranteed access to the law and to the courts to defend their legally protected rights and interests, and justice cannot be denied for lack of economic conditions,[19] as several obstacles to access to justice have been identified, including economic obstacles.[20] Second, everyone has the right, under the terms of the law, to legal information and consultation, to legal representation and to be accompanied by a lawyer before any authority.[21] Third, everyone has the right to have a case in which they intervene be decided within a reasonable period of time and through a fair process.[22] Fourth, for the defence of citizen's rights, freedoms and personal guarantees, the law guarantees judicial procedures characterized by speed and priority in order to obtain effective and timely protection against threats or protection of these rights.[23]

37. Moreover, Portugal is a party to international human rights treaties, which further protect individuals' rights in civil matters. These treaties contribute to the interpretation and application of civil justice guarantees. In particular, the European Convention on Human Rights (EConHR)[24] provides the right to a fair trial, according to which:

> In the determination of his civil rights and obligations or of any criminal charge against him, everyone is entitled to a fair and public hearing within a reasonable time by an independent and impartial tribunal established by law. Judgment shall be pronounced publicly but the press and public may be excluded from all or part of the trial in the interests of morals, public order or national security in a democratic society, where the interests of juveniles or the protection of the private life of the parties so require, or to the extent strictly necessary in the opinion of the court in special circumstances where publicity would prejudice the interests of justice.[25]

38. The right to a fair trial provided by the EConHR is an integral part of Portuguese law concerning the relationship between national law and international

---

18. STJ judgment of 19 Mar. 2019, Case No. 30531/16.4YIPRT.L1.S1, www.dgsi.pt.
19. Article 20(1) of the Constitution.
20. Law No. 34/2004 of 29 July amends the regime of access to the law and courts and implements into the internal legal system Council Directive No. 2003/8/EC, of 27 January, on improving access to justice in cross-border disputes through the establishment of common minimum rules regarding legal aid in the context of such disputes.
21. Article 20(2) of the Constitution.
22. Article 20(4) of the Constitution.
23. Article 20(5) of the Constitution.
24. Available at https://www.echr.coe.int/documents/guide_art_6_criminal_eng.pdf.
25. Article 6 of the EConHR.

law.[26] The right to a fair trial is an essential feature of the constitutional principle of the rule of law: 'The Portuguese Republic is a democratic State based on the rule of law, based on popular sovereignty, pluralism of expression and democratic political organization, respect and the guarantee of the realization of fundamental rights and freedoms and the separation and interdependence of powers (…)'.[27]

39. Moreover, Portugal is a Member State of the EU and, therefore, Portuguese citizens also have the rights provided by the Charter of Fundamental Rights of the European Union (Charter),[28] including the right to an effective remedy and to a fair trial, according to which: 'Everyone whose rights and freedoms guaranteed by the law of the Union are violated has the right to an effective remedy before a tribunal in compliance with the conditions laid down in this Article. / Everyone is entitled to a fair and public hearing within a reasonable time by an independent and impartial tribunal previously established by law. Everyone shall have the possibility of being advised, defended and represented. / Legal aid shall be made available to those who lack sufficient resources in so far as such aid is necessary to ensure effective access to justice.'[29]

40. Fundamental guarantees in civil proceedings mean establishment of courts by law, independence and impartiality of judges, reasoned decisions, publicity of proceedings, fair trial, reasonable time of decisions, and guarantees of appeal.

41. The courts in Portugal are established and organized by law. This ensures the proper functioning and structure of the judiciary, including the allocation of jurisdiction and the creation of specialized courts. The Constitution provides that the courts are sovereign bodies with the competence to administer justice on behalf of the people, ensuring the defence of the legally protected rights and interests of citizens, repressing violations of democratic legality and resolving conflicts of public and private interests.[30] Moreover, the courts are independent and subject only to the law, and they cannot apply norms that infringe on the provisions of the Constitution or the principles enshrined therein.[31]

42. Independence and impartiality are keystones of the courts, as judges in civil matters are expected to exercise their functions independently and impartially. They should be free from external influences or pressures that could undermine their ability to make fair and unbiased decisions.

43. Then, judicial decisions in civil matters must be reasoned, meaning that judges are required to provide a clear explanation of the legal and factual basis for their rulings. This allows parties to understand the rationale behind the decision and

26. Article 8 of the Constitution.
27. Article 2 of the Constitution.
28. Available at https://eur-lex.europa.eu/legal-content/EN/TXT/?uri=CELEX:12012P/TXT.
29. Article 47 of the Charter of Fundamental Rights in the Union.
30. Article 202(1) and (2) of the Constitution.
31. Articles 203 and 204 of the Constitution.

facilitate potential appeals. The decisions of the courts (except those of mere expediency) are based on the law, binding on all public and private entities, and prevail over those of any other authorities.[32]

44. Moreover, civil proceedings in Portugal are generally open to the public, ensuring transparency and accountability. However, certain cases may be subject to restrictions on publicity to protect sensitive information or privacy rights. Court hearings are public, except when the court itself decides otherwise, in a reasoned order, to safeguard the dignity of persons and public morals or to guarantee its normal functioning.[33]

45. Parties involved in civil matters have the right to a fair trial, which includes the right to be heard, present their case, challenge evidence, and have their claims adjudicated in accordance with the law. The principle of equality of arms ensures that both parties have an equal opportunity to present their arguments and evidence.

46. Civil proceedings should be conducted in a reasonable time frame to prevent undue delays and ensure effective access to justice. This guarantees that individuals can have their disputes resolved within a reasonable period.

47. Finally, parties have the right to appeal decisions of lower courts to higher instances. This allows for a review of the case by a higher judicial authority and provides an opportunity for correction or reconsideration of errors or points of law.

48. These fundamental guarantees collectively uphold the principles of fairness, access to justice, and the protection of individuals' rights within the Portuguese civil justice system. They contribute to maintaining the rule of law and ensuring the proper functioning of the civil courts.

III. General Principles of Civil Procedure

49. The CPC provides a set of basic principles which lay down the foundations of civil procedure law, such as the guarantee of access to courts (and the prohibition of self-defence), the adversarial principle (claim and contradictory), equality of the parties, procedural management, cooperation, good faith, mutual correction, and the use of simple and clear language.

50. To begin with, the State guarantees access to courts, i.e., legal protection through the courts, so that everyone has the right to obtain, within a reasonable period of time, a judicial decision that assesses, with the force of res judicata, the claim regularly raised in court, as well as the possibility of having it executed.[34] The guarantee of access to courts is critical because no one is allowed to resort to force

32. Article 205(1) and (2) of the Constitution.
33. Article 206 of the Constitution.
34. Article 2(1) CPC.

in order to realize or to ensure their own right, except in cases and within the limits established by law.[35] According to the rule laid down in the CC, it is lawful to resort to force in order to carry out or ensure one's right when the direct action is pending due to the impossibility of continuing the normal coercive means in good time, to avoid the practical destruction of that right, provided that the agent does not exceed whatever is necessary to avoid harm.[36] Direct action, which may consist in the appropriation, destruction or deterioration of a thing, in the elimination of irregularly opposed resistance to the exercise of the right, or in another similar act, must be proportionate because it is not lawful when it sacrifices interests that prevail over those that the agent seeks to achieve or ensure.[37]

51. Procedural terms are instrumental to substantive law, meaning that procedure is designed after the nature and features of each 'substantive right'. As the STJ puts it, 'Civil procedure must be seen in its adjective role in relation to the objective of fair composition of the dispute.'[38]

52. The principle is that for every right, there is a corresponding appropriate action to make it recognized in court, to prevent or repair its violation and to enforce it coercively, as well as there are the necessary procedures to safeguard the useful effect of the action.[39]

53. Moreover, civil procedure is governed by dispositive ('dispositivo') and adversarial principles (claim and contradictory). It means that the court cannot resolve the conflict of interests that the action presupposes without the resolution being requested by one of the parties and the other being duly called to present opposition, as only in the exceptional cases provided for by law measures can be taken against a certain person without that person being previously heard.[40] The adversarial principle, which must be observed and enforced throughout the entire process, prevents judges from deciding questions of law or fact without the parties having had the opportunity to comment on them, except in the case of manifesting unnecessary need.[41] The adversarial principle requires respect for the definition of the dispute made by the parties so that if the Court decides on an issue that the parties did not raise, the ruling is subject to partial nullity due to excessive pronouncement.[42]

54. Whether bringing or contesting a claim, it is up to the parties to allege the essential facts that constitute the cause of action and those on which the invoked

35. Article 1 CPC.
36. Article 336(1) of the CC.
37. Article 326(2) and (3) of the CC.
38. STJ judgment of 19 Jun. 2019, Case No. 7439/16.8T8STB.E1.S1, www.dgsi.pt.
39. Article 2(2) CPC.
40. Article 3(1) and (2) CPC.
41. Article 3(3) CPC.
42. Article 615(1)(d) CPC, and STJ judgment of 24 Jan. 2019, Case No. 1250/12.2TBVCD-A.P1.S1, www.dgsi.pt.

exceptions are based.[43] Despite judges being bound to the facts carried into proceedings by the parties, they can also consider instrumental or complementary facts, as well as well-known facts and those of which the court is aware by virtue of the exercise of its functions.[44] However, concerning legal issues – i.e., investigation, interpretation and application of the rules of law – the judge is not subject to the allegations of the parties.[45]

55. Another principle of civil procedure is equality of the parties, which means that the court must ensure, throughout the entire process, a status of substantial equality of the parties, namely in the exercise of faculties, in the use of means of defence and in the application of commissions or procedural sanctions.[46] Looking after the equality of the parties is part of the judge's general duty of procedural management, meaning that he must actively direct the process and ensure that it proceeds swiftly, promoting the necessary steps for the normal continuation of the action, refusing what is impertinent or merely dilatory and, after hearing the parties, adopting procedural simplification and streamlining mechanisms that guarantee the fair composition of the dispute within a reasonable time.[47] In particular, the judge officiously provides for the supply of the lack of procedural assumptions susceptible to remedy, determining the performance of the acts necessary for the regularization of the instance or when the remedy depends on an act that must be practised by the parties, inviting them to practice it.[48]

56. Besides judges, other participants in the process are subject to general procedural duties under, for instance, the principle of cooperation, according to which, when conducting and intervening in the process, magistrates, legal representatives and the parties themselves must cooperate with each other, contributing to obtain, with brevity and efficiency, the fair composition of the dispute.[49] In special, as the judge may, at any time during the proceedings, hear the parties, their representatives or legal representatives, she can invite them to provide clarifications on matters of fact or law that appear to be relevant and inform the other party of the due diligence results, and those persons are obliged to appear whenever they are notified to do so and, in principle, to provide the clarifications requested of them.[50] In particular, upon the parties lies a duty of procedural good faith: they must act in good faith and observe those duties of cooperation,[51] and all persons, whether or not they are parties to the cause, have the duty to collaborate in the discovery of the truth, answering whatever is asked of them, submitting to the necessary inspections,

43. Article 5 CPC.
44. Article 5(2) CPC.
45. Article 5(3) CPC. Articles 5 to 13 of the Civil Code provide guidelines on the interpretation of laws, including resorting to *analogia legis* and *analogia iuris* to fill gaps of statutory law.
46. Article 4 CPC.
47. Article 6(1) CPC.
48. Article 6(2) CPC.
49. Article 7(1) CPC.
50. Article 7(2) and (3) CPC.
51. Article 8 CPC.

providing whatever is requested and practising the acts that are determined.[52] Refusal of due collaboration is sanctioned by a fine, and if the refusing person is a party, the court freely assesses the value of the refusal for evidence purposes.[53] Reasons for legitimate refusal include physical or moral integrity of persons, privacy, and professional or State secrecy.[54]

57. A general duty of mutual correction applies to all those involved in the procedure. It means in special that a special duty of courtesy guides the relations between lawyers and magistrates and that neither party shall use, in its writings or oral arguments, expressions that are unnecessarily or unjustifiably offensive to the honour or good name of the other, or to the respect due to the institutions,[55] under penalty of 'contempt of court'.

58. Finally, it is also a procedural principle that the courts preferably use simple and clear language in all their acts, in particular in citations, notifications and other communications addressed directly to the parties and other natural and legal persons.[56]

IV. Main Issues in Discussion

59. Some issues and trends in Portuguese civil procedure can be pointed out, reflecting the ongoing efforts to improve access to justice, enhance procedural efficiency, and adapt to the changing legal landscape.

60. Ensuring access to justice for all individuals, regardless of their economic means or social status, is a central concern. This includes exploring mechanisms to reduce the costs of litigation, providing legal aid and assistance, and promoting alternative dispute resolution methods as viable options for resolving disputes.

61. There is an ongoing discussion about the need to continue to simplify and streamline civil procedure in order to make it more accessible, efficient, and cost-effective. This includes measures to reduce the complexity of procedural rules, expedite proceedings, and promote alternative dispute resolution methods.

62. In particular, the digitalization of court proceedings includes the use of electronic filing systems, digital communication channels, and electronic evidence management. The effective integration of technology into civil procedure raises issues related to data protection, security, and the need for appropriate infrastructure and training. The use of AI systems in civil proceedings is also a matter of discussion and concern. For instance, the proposed Regulation on AI in Europe provides that

52. Article 417(1) CPC.
53. Article 417(2) CPC.
54. Article 417(3) CPC.
55. Article 9(1) and (2) CPC.
56. Article 9-A CPC.

AI systems intended to assist a judicial authority in researching and interpreting facts and the law and in applying the law to a concrete set of facts are considered high-risk AI systems,[57] and therefore it justifies precautionary rules and control on risk management system, data and data governance, technical documentation, record-keeping, transparency and provision of information to users, human oversight, and accuracy, robustness and cybersecurity. According to Recital (40) as amended by the European Parliament:

> (40) Certain AI systems intended for the administration of justice and democratic processes should be classified as high-risk, considering their potentially significant impact on democracy, rule of law, individual freedoms as well as the right to an effective remedy and to a fair trial. In particular, to address the risks of potential biases, errors and opacity, it is appropriate to qualify as high-risk AI systems intended to ***be used by a judicial authority or administrative body or on their behalf to*** assist judicial authorities ***or administrative bodies*** in researching and interpreting facts and the law and in applying the law to a concrete set of facts ***or used in a similar way in alternative dispute resolution. The use of artificial intelligence tools can support, but should not replace the decision-making power of judges or judicial independence, as the final decision-making must remain a human-driven activity and decision***. Such qualification should not extend, however, to AI systems intended for purely ancillary administrative activities that do not affect the actual administration of justice in individual cases, such as anonymisation or pseudonymisation of judicial decisions, documents or data, communication between personnel, administrative tasks or allocation of resources.[58]

63. Nonetheless, AI systems may actually help judges with their role in actively managing cases and controlling the progress of proceedings, including setting trial dates, managing evidence, and ensuring procedural fairness while avoiding unnecessary delays and formalities.

64. The effectiveness and efficiency of enforcement proceedings to ensure compliance with court judgments is also an important issue, including both the enforcement of domestic judgments and the recognition and enforcement of foreign judgments.

65. The promotion and development of alternative dispute resolution methods, such as mediation and arbitration, are increasingly important in Portuguese civil procedure. There is a focus on encouraging parties to consider these methods as alternatives to traditional court litigation, particularly in resolving certain types of

57. Proposal for a Regulation of the European Parliament and of the Council Laying Down Harmonised Rules on Artificial Intelligence (Artificial Intelligence Act) and Amending Certain Union Legislative Acts, COM(2021) 206 final, Article 6(2) and Annex III, para. 8(a).
58. Amendments adopted by the European Parliament on 14 Jun. 2023 on the proposal for a regulation of the European Parliament and of the Council on laying down harmonised rules on artificial intelligence (Artificial Intelligence Act) and amending certain Union legislative acts https://www.europarl.europa.eu/doceo/document/TA-9-2023-0236_EN.html.

disputes. For instance, based on EU law on alternative resolution of consumer disputes, there are several out-of-court settlement mechanisms for consumer disputes.[59]

66. In order to guarantee the right of access to the courts to consumers, it is important to mention the EU Directive on representative actions for the protection of the collective interests of consumers.[60] This Directive represents a very important step in the protection of European consumers insofar as, through the mechanisms of injunction and reparation, consumers can enforce their rights at the European level. Unlike Portugal, which, since 1985, has had mechanisms for redress through popular and injunctive actions for consumer rights' infringements, in some Member States, such mechanisms were not contemplated. This Directive ensures that, in all Member States of the EU, a system of collective actions is in force to protect the collective interests of consumers against violations of Union Law.

67. With a broad scope of application, this Directive covers areas such as financial services, travel and tourism, energy, health, telecommunications and data protection. The action mechanisms may be used on behalf of consumers by qualified entities, which must be designated in advance by the Member States. Harmonized eligibility criteria are established for qualified entities for the purposes of bringing cross-border actions, and Member States are free to establish designation criteria for those entities for purposes of domestic actions. The transposition deadline was twenty-four months from the entry into force of the Directive. However, the Directive does not interfere with existing national collective action systems, such as the one provided by the legislation on Popular Action[61] and Consumer Protection,[62] according to which procedural standing to enforce consumers' rights is recognized to consumers who are directly injured, as well as, under the terms of Law No. 83/95 of 31 August (popular action), to consumers and consumer associations, even if they are not directly injured.[63]

59. Enacted by Law No. 144/2015 of 8 September (implements Directive 2013/11/EU, of the European Parliament and of the Council, of 21 May 2013, on the alternative resolution of consumer disputes, and repeals the Decrees-Law No. 146/99 of 4 May and No. 60/2011 of 6 May), as last amended by Decree-Law No. 9/2021 of 29 January.
60. Directive (EU) 2020/1828 of the European Parliament and of the Council of 25 Nov. 2020 on representative actions for the protection of the collective interests of consumers and repealing Directive 2009/22/EC.
61. Enacted by Law No. 83/95 of 31 August ('direito de participação procedimental e de acção popular'), as last amended by Decree-Law No. 214-G/2015 of 2 October.
62. Enacted by Law No. 24/96 of 31 July ('Lei de defesa do consumidor'), as last amended by Law No. 28/2023 of 4 July.
63. Article 13 of Law No. 24/96 of 31 July. The Public Prosecutor's Office and the Directorate-General for Consumer Affairs also have standing when individual homogeneous, collective or diffuse interests are at stake.

Part I. Judicial Organization

Chapter 1. The Courts and Their Members

§1. Courts

I. Structure of the Court System

68. The courts are sovereign bodies with competence to administer justice on behalf of the people (the so-called jurisdictional function), to ensure the defence of legally protected rights and interests, to repress violations of democratic legality and to resolve conflicts of public and private interests.[64]

69. The court system in Portugal is organized into several levels, each with its specific jurisdiction and responsibilities. The Constitution provides that there are several categories of courts:[65] (1) the Constitutional Court (TC); (2) civil courts, including Courts of First Instance, Courts of Appeal and the STJ; (3) the Supreme Administrative Court and other administrative and tax courts; and (4) the Court of Auditors ('Tribunal de Contas'). The Constitution also provides the possibility for other courts, notably maritime courts, arbitration tribunals and justices of peace ('julgados de paz').[66] The Statute on the Organization of the Judicial System[67] governs the court system in Portugal.

70. The TC ('Tribunal Constitucional') is the highest court for constitutional matters in Portugal. It is responsible for reviewing the constitutionality of laws and resolving constitutional disputes. It consists of thirteen judges co-opted and appointed by various entities:[68] ten are elected by the Assembly of the Republic by a qualified majority, and the remaining three are co-opted by the elected judges, also by qualified majority. At least six must be chosen from among judges of the other courts and the rest from among jurists. The term of office of constitutional judges lasts for nine years and is not renewable, and the exercise of disciplinary power over the judges of the TC rests with the President, with appeal to the Court itself.

64. Article 202 of the Constitution and Article 2 of the Judicial System Organization Statute, enacted by Law No. 62/2013 of 26 August, as last amended by Law No. 77/2021 of 23 November.
65. Article 209 of the Constitution.
66. Articles 210 to 214 of the Constitution.
67. 'Lei da Organização do Sistema Judiciário' (LOSJ), enacted by Law No. 62/2013 of 26 August.
68. Article 222 of the Constitution. *See also* the Act on the organization, operation and procedure of the TC, approved by Law No. 28/82 of 15 November.

71. The STJ ('Supremo Tribunal de Justiça') is the highest court for ordinary civil and criminal matters. In principle, the STJ only hears matters of law, exercises jurisdiction over appeals and cassation processes from lower courts, and comprises multiple divisions specialized in different areas of law, including civil, criminal, and social (labour).[69]

72. The Supreme Administrative Court ('Supremo Tribunal Administrativo') is the highest court for administrative and fiscal matters. It handles appeals related to administrative disputes, tax matters, and administrative liability and consists of multiple divisions specializing in administrative and tax law.[70]

73. The Court of Auditors ('Tribunal de Contas') is responsible for auditing and overseeing the management of public funds. It reviews the legality and regularity of public expenditures and public accounts and ensures financial accountability of public entities and public officials.[71]

74. The Courts of Appeal ('Tribunal da Relação') are intermediate appellate courts located in different regions of Portugal. They hear appeals from lower courts, including judgments from district courts and specialized courts, and are divided into five regional Courts of Appeal, each covering a specific geographical area (Coimbra, Évora, Guimarães, Lisboa, Porto). The Courts of Appeal comprise sections in civil matters, criminal matters, social matters, matters of family and minors, matters of commerce and matters of intellectual property and competition, regulation and supervision.[72]

75. Courts of First Instance are, in principle, district courts ('tribunais de comarca'). They have general jurisdiction spread throughout Portugal, handle a wide range of civil, criminal, labour, and family law cases and may consist of multiple divisions or sections specialized in different areas of law. Courts of First Instance include courts with extended territorial jurisdiction and district courts, and for this purpose, the national territory is divided into twenty-three districts ('comarcas'). Several courts of specialized jurisdiction may be created, such as 'central civil, 'local cível', 'central criminal', 'local criminal', 'local of small criminality', 'instrução criminal', 'family and minors', 'labour', 'trade' and 'execution.'[73]

69. Articles 46 and 47 of the Judicial System Organization Statute, enacted by Law No. 62/2013 of 26 August.
70. Article 146 of Judicial System Organization Statute, enacted by Law No. 62/2013 of 26 August. *See* the Administrative and Tax Courts Statute, enacted by Law No. 13/2002 of 19 February, as last amended by Law No. 114/2019 of 12 September.
71. *See* the Statute on the Organization and Procedure of the Court of Auditors, enacted by Law No. 98/97 of 26 August, as last amended by Law No. 12/2022 of 27 June.
72. Article 67 of the Judicial System Organization Statute, enacted by Law No. 62/2013 of 26 August.
73. Articles 33 and 81 of Judicial System Organization Statute (LOSJ).

76. Administrative and Tax Courts ('Tribunais Administrativos e Fiscais') are specialized courts responsible for resolving administrative and tax disputes. These courts deal with cases related to administrative acts, public procurement, taxation, and administrative offences.[74]

77. In addition to these courts, there may be specialized courts, such as maritime courts, as well arbitration courts and the so-called justices of peace (julgados de paz).[75] In 'justices of peace',[76] procedural requirements are simplified. The parties may submit their cases orally and the disputes may be solved through mediation, conciliation or through a court hearing. If the agreement is not reached through mediation, the judge tries the conciliation, and if it is not successful, there is a hearing before the court to hear the parties, produce evidence and deliver a sentence by the judge. Justices of peace have jurisdiction on civil declarative actions, the value of which does not exceed EUR 15,000, excluding proceedings on matters of family law matters, successions and labour law. Justices of peace decisions, which do not exceed half the value of the threshold of Courts of First Instance (EUR 2,500), can be appealed before the district court where the justice of peace is located.

II. Administration of the Court

78. The administration of the court system in Portugal is primarily overseen by the Ministry of Justice ('Ministério da Justiça'). The ministry is responsible for the overall coordination, organization, and management of the judicial system in the country.[77]

79. The Ministry of Justice and related institutions play a crucial role in ensuring the smooth functioning and effective administration of the court system in the country, which also involves the implementation of digital technologies to enhance efficiency and accessibility. The country has been implementing e-justice initiatives to digitize court processes, improve communication, and provide online access to legal information and services.

80. Some key aspects of court administration in Portugal include the Supreme Council of the Judiciary ('Conselho Superior da Magistratura'), the Directorate-General for Justice Administration ('Direção-Geral da Administração da Justiça'), Judicial Magistrates (Bench) and Public Prosecutors (and ('Ministério Público).

81. The High Council of the Judiciary ('Conselho Superior da Magistratura'[78]) is an independent body responsible for overseeing the judicial system. The main

74. *See* the Administrative and Tax Courts Statute, enacted by Law No. 13/2002 of 19 February, as last amended by Law No. 114/2019 of 12 September.
75. Article 209(2) of the Constitution.
76. Statute on the organization, competence and functioning of the Justice of Peace enacted by Law No. 78/2001, of 13 July, as amended by the Law No. 54/2013, of 31 July.
77. https://justica.gov.pt/.
78. https://www.csm.org.pt/.

functions of the Council include the appointment, promotion, transfer, and disciplinary proceedings of judges, and it ensures the proper functioning and efficiency of the courts. The High Council of the Judiciary is composed of the President of the STJ, two members appointed by the President of the Republic, seven elected by the Assembly of the Republic, seven elected by the Judicial Magistrates (one being a judge of the STJ who exercises functions of Vice-President, two Judges of the Courts of Appeal and four Judges of Law, one proposed by each judicial district). The High Council for the Judiciary also includes the Secretary Judge, appointed from among the Judges of Law.[79]

82. The Directorate-General for Justice Administration ('Direção-Geral da Administração da Justiça') is a department under the Ministry of Justice. It supports the administrative management of the courts, ensuring the proper functioning of judicial services. The directorate is responsible for matters such as court organization, human resources, budgeting, and infrastructure.[80]

83. Magistrates, including judges and prosecutors, play a crucial role in the administration of justice. Court personnel, such as court clerks and administrative staff, assist in the day-to-day functioning of the courts.[81]

84. The Judiciary Police[82] ('Polícia Judiciária'[83]) is a specialized law enforcement agency in Portugal. It works closely with the courts and judicial magistrates to investigate and gather evidence in criminal cases.

85. The Bar Association ('Ordem dos Advogados'[84]) is an independent professional organization for lawyers in Portugal. It promotes professional ethics, regulates the legal profession, and provides support and representation for lawyers.[85] It is a matter of constitutional law that lawyers are statutorily guaranteed the necessary immunities to exercise their mandate and that legal representation is an essential element in the administration of justice.[86]

III. Bench and 'Ministère Public'/Public Prosecutors in Portugal

86. The Portuguese judicial system involves both a Bench, which comprises judges, and a Public Prosecutor's Office, which represents the State. The Public

79. Articles 217 and 218 of the Constitution.
80. https://dgaj.justica.gov.pt/.
81. *See* Statute of Court Clerks ('Estatuto dos Oficiais de Justiça'), enacted by Decree-law No. 343/99 of 26 August (several times amended).
82. The organic Statute of the judiciary police was enacted by Decree-Law No. 14/2010 of 15 November.
83. https://www.policiajudiciaria.pt/.
84. https://portal.oa.pt/.
85. Statute of the Portuguese Bar Association, enacted by Law No. 145/2015 of 8 September, and as last amended by Law No. 79/2021 of 24 November.
86. Article 208 of the Constitution.

Prosecutor's Office is part of the judicial system, but it is a distinct entity from the Bench. Judges and public prosecutors have separate roles and responsibilities, but they collaborate to uphold the rule of law and administer justice in Portugal.

87. The Bench ('Magistratura Judicial')[87] consists of judges who preside over cases and render judicial decisions. Judges are independent and impartial and are responsible for interpreting and applying the law. They ensure fair and equitable proceedings, protect individual rights and administer justice in accordance with the law.

88. The Public Prosecutor's Office ('Ministério Público')[88] is an independent entity responsible for representing the public interest and ensuring the proper application of the law. It is headed by the Attorney General of the Republic ('Procurador-Geral da República') and operates at different levels, including the national, regional, and local levels. Public prosecutors ('Magistrados do Ministério Público') are responsible for prosecuting criminal cases, supervising investigations, and defending the public interest in legal proceedings. They act as the voice of the prosecution, presenting evidence and arguments in court.

89. The relationship between the Bench and the Public Prosecutor's Office is essential for the functioning of the Portuguese judicial system. Public prosecutors play a significant role in ensuring the proper enforcement of the law, protecting the rights of individuals, and representing the public interest in legal proceedings. They work closely with judges to ensure fair and impartial trials.

IV. Appointment of Judges and Public Prosecutors

90. The appointment of judges, public prosecutors, and members of the Public Prosecutor's Office ('Ministério Público') follows a specific process.

91. Judges ('Magistratura Judicial') are appointed by the High Council for the Judiciary ('Conselho Superior da Magistratura'). This Council is responsible for the selection, appointment, transfer, promotion, and disciplinary proceedings of judges. The composition and functions of this Council are defined by law[89] to safeguard the independence of the judiciary and ensure transparency and accountability in the selection process. The Council is composed of judges and other members, ensuring a balanced representation. The appointment process involves open competitions, where candidates are evaluated based on their qualifications, professional experience, and suitability for judicial roles.

---

87. Statute of Judges ('Magistrados Judiciais'), enacted by Law No. 21/85 of 30 July, as last amended by Law No. 2/2020 of 31 March.
88. Article 219 of the Constitution and Statute of the Public Prosecutor enacted by Law No. 68/2019 of 27 August.
89. Statute of Judges ('Magistrados Judiciais'), enacted by Law No. 21/85 of 30 July.

92. Public Prosecutors ('Magistratura do Ministério Público') are appointed by the Attorney General of the Republic through the High Council of the Public Prosecutor.[90] The Council follows a rigorous procedure for the selection, appointment, transfer, promotion, and disciplinary proceedings of public prosecutors. Candidates for the Public Prosecutor's Office go through an examination process, which assesses their legal knowledge, skills, and aptitude for the position.

93. The appointment process aims to ensure the independence and impartiality of judges and the autonomy of public prosecutors, promoting a fair and efficient judicial system. It seeks to select qualified individuals who demonstrate competence, integrity, and a commitment to upholding the rule of law.

§2. Members of the Judiciary

I. Incompatibilities

94. Members of the judiciary are subject to certain incompatibilities to ensure the independence, impartiality, and integrity of the judicial system. These incompatibilities restrict the activities and engagements of judges and aim to prevent conflicts of interest.

95. The Constitution expressly prevents acting judges from carrying out any other public or private function, except unpaid law teaching or scientific research, and from being appointed to service commissions outside the scope of the courts without authorization from the High Council, without prejudice to other incompatibilities established by law.[91] Copyright payments for the production or publication of literary or artistic work are not prohibited.[92] Several judges have published very important books on civil procedure law, providing relevant contributions to the understanding and enforcement of law not only 'in the books' but also 'in action'.

96. Common incompatibilities for members of the judiciary include prohibition of political activities, limitations on outside employment, financial interests and investments, restrictions on public commentary, and limitations on social relationships.

97. To begin with, judges are generally prohibited from engaging in political activities, such as holding political office, participating in political campaigns, or joining political organizations. This restriction helps maintain the impartiality and neutrality of judges in their decision-making. Then, judges are usually restricted from engaging in other paid employment or holding positions outside their judicial role. This restriction aims to prevent conflicts of interest and ensure that judges can

90. Articles 219 and 220 of the Constitution.
91. Article 216(3) to (5) of the Constitution.
92. Article 8-A of the Statute of Judges ('Magistrados Judiciais'), enacted by Law No. 21/85 of 30 July.

dedicate themselves fully to their judicial duties. Moreover, judges are required to avoid any financial interests or investments that may compromise their independence, impartiality, or integrity. This includes refraining from investments or financial activities that could create a conflict of interest or give the appearance of bias in their judicial decisions.

98. Furthermore, judges are expected to exercise caution when publicly expressing their views, especially on matters that may come before them in court. This helps maintain the perception of impartiality and avoids potential prejudice in ongoing or future cases. Judges may also be required to maintain a certain level of discretion in their social relationships to avoid potential conflicts of interest or perceptions of bias. This includes refraining from close personal relationships with individuals who may have a direct or indirect interest in cases over which they preside.

99. These incompatibilities aim to uphold the principles of independence, impartiality, and integrity within the judiciary. They help maintain public trust and confidence in the judicial system by ensuring that judges can carry out their duties with fairness and objectivity. Specific rules and regulations regarding incompatibilities for members of the judiciary are provided by the Statute of Judges as well as by the Code of Conduct adopted in 2020 by the High Council for the Judiciary.[93]

II. End of Functions

100. The end of functions of the judiciary in Portugal refers to the termination or conclusion of a judge's tenure or term of office. As a constitutional rule, except where statutorily provided for, judges are irremovable and cannot be transferred, suspended, retired or dismissed, and they cannot be held responsible for their decisions.[94]

101. Notwithstanding, there are several circumstances under which the functions of a judge in Portugal may come to an end,[95] such as retirement, resignation, disciplinary measures and term limits.

102. To begin with, judges in Portugal have a mandatory retirement age, which is typically set at 70 years old. When a judge reaches retirement age, they cease to hold their judicial functions and may enter into retirement. Then, a judge may choose to voluntarily resign from their position, ending their functions as a member of the judiciary. Resignation typically requires submitting a formal letter of resignation to the appropriate authorities. Disciplinary measures may be another cause

93. https://www.csm.org.pt/2020/07/07/codigo-de-conduta/.
94. Article 216(1) and (2) of the Constitution.
95. Articles 70 *et seq.* of the Statute of Judges ('Magistrados Judiciais'), enacted by Law No. 21/85 of 30 July.

for the end of functions: in cases where a judge is found to have committed serious misconduct or ethical breaches, disciplinary measures may be imposed. Depending on the severity of the misconduct, disciplinary actions can range from temporary suspension to permanent removal from the judiciary. Finally, in certain positions within the judiciary, such as the President of the STJ or the Attorney General of the Republic, there are term limits in place. For example, the President of the STJ is elected for a single term of five years.[96] At the end of their designated term, the functions of these high-ranking judicial officials come to an end.

103. It's important to note that the end of a judge's functions does not necessarily mean the end of their involvement in the legal field. After retiring or resigning, judges may pursue other legal activities such as private practice, teaching, or serving in advisory roles.

III. Discipline

104. In Portugal, the discipline of members of the judiciary is governed by specific rules and procedures to ensure accountability, uphold the integrity of the judicial system, and maintain public trust. The discipline of members of the judiciary involves the investigation and resolution of complaints and misconduct allegations.

105. The High Council for the Judiciary ('Conselho Superior da Magistratura') is the body responsible for overseeing the discipline of members of the judiciary. It has the authority to investigate and decide on disciplinary proceedings against judges and public prosecutors.[97]

106. Disciplinary investigations are initiated when a complaint or allegation of misconduct is made against a judge. The High Council for the Judiciary carries out an investigation to examine the merits of the complaint and gather evidence. If the investigation finds evidence of misconduct, the High Council for the Judiciary may impose disciplinary measures, which can range from a warning or reprimand to more severe penalties, such as suspension or removal from office. The severity of the measure depends on the nature and seriousness of the misconduct.

107. Disciplinary proceedings involve a formal process where the accused member of the judiciary has the opportunity to present their defence. The proceedings may include hearings, the examination of witnesses and evidence, and the consideration of legal arguments. Decisions on disciplinary measures made by the High Council for the Judiciary can be subject to appeal. Appeals are typically heard by the STJ, which reviews the legality and fairness of the disciplinary decision. The

96. Article 61(1) of the Judicial System Organization Statute (LOSJ), enacted by Law No. 62/2013 of 26 August.
97. Articles 81 *et seq.* of the Statute of Judges ('Estatuto dos Magistrados Judiciais'), enacted by Law No. 21/85 of 30 July.

disciplinary process for members of the judiciary in Portugal is designed to ensure due process, fairness, and transparency. By enforcing disciplinary measures, Portugal seeks to maintain high standards of professionalism, ethics, and integrity within the judiciary and uphold public confidence in the administration of justice.

Chapter 2. The Bar

§1. Exercise of the Legal Profession (Conditions for Admission, Rights and Duties, Discipline)

108. The exercise of the legal profession in Portugal is regulated and overseen by the Bar Association ('Ordem dos Advogados'[98]). The Bar Association is an independent professional organization with its own Statute[99] that represents and regulates lawyers in Portugal. Some key regulatory aspects regarding the exercise of the legal profession in Portugal include admission to the Bar, compliance with the Code of Ethics and Professional Conduct, professional practice, continuing legal education, and disciplinary proceedings.

109. To practice law in Portugal, individuals must be admitted to the Bar Association. Admission requirements include holding a law degree from a recognized institution, completing a traineeship period, and passing the Bar Association's examination. Then, the Bar Association enforces deontological rules of ethics and professional conduct that lawyers must adhere to in their practice. The code sets standards for professional integrity, confidentiality, loyalty to clients, and the duty to act in the best interests of justice.[100]

110. The Bar Association has the authority to initiate disciplinary proceedings against lawyers who are alleged to have violated the code of ethics or engaged in professional misconduct. Disciplinary measures can range from warnings and fines to temporary suspension or even disbarment. The Bar Association plays a crucial role in regulating and upholding professional standards within the legal profession in Portugal. It aims to ensure the competence, integrity, and ethical conduct of lawyers while safeguarding the interests of clients and the public.

111. Lawyers in Portugal can engage in various areas of legal practice, including advising clients, representing them in court, and providing legal assistance and representation in administrative, civil, criminal, and commercial matters. The law defines a set of acts which can only be carried out by lawyers,[101] who can work as self-employed practitioners or be members of law firms. Law firms cannot adopt the commercial form, but only one of two special (civil) types, and the signature of the contract must mention the adopted regime: unlimited liability companies ('RI'), or limited liability companies ('RL').[102]

---

98. https://portal.oa.pt/.
99. Statute of the Bar Association, enacted by Law No. 145/2015 of 8 September, and as last amended by Law No. 79/2021 of 24 November.
100. Articles 88 *et seq.* Statute of the Bar Association enacted by Law No. 145/2015 of 8 September.
101. Acts of Lawyers Statute, enacted by Law No. 49/2004 of 24 August ('Lei dos Actos Próprios dos Advogados').
102. Article 213 of Statute of the Bar Association. See also the Statute on the Creation, Organization and Operation of Professional Public Associations, enacted by Law No. 2/2013 of 10 January.

112. Finally, the Bar Association promotes continuing legal education to ensure that lawyers stay updated on legal developments and maintain their professional competence. Lawyers are encouraged to participate in training programmes, seminars, and other educational activities to enhance their knowledge and skills.

§2. (PUBLIC) INSTITUTIONS AND (PRIVATE) ORGANIZATIONS

113. The legal profession involves both public institutions and private organizations that play distinct roles in the regulation and practice of law. The key institutions and organizations related to the legal profession in Portugal include the Bar Association, the Courts, the Ministry of Justice, the Attorney General's Office, Registry Offices, Notaries, Law Firms and other legal organizations. These institutions and organizations collectively contribute to the functioning of the legal profession in Portugal, ensuring the delivery of justice, regulation of lawyers and solicitors, and the provision of legal services to individuals, businesses, and the public. Each institution has its specific responsibilities and functions within the legal system, with a balance between public oversight and private legal practice.

114. The Court system in Portugal consists of various judicial bodies responsible for the administration of justice. The Courts ('Tribunais') include the TC, the STJ, Administrative and Tax Courts, Judicial Courts, and others. These courts operate as public institutions, with judges appointed through the judicial system and responsible for adjudicating legal disputes.

115. The Bar Association ('Ordem dos Advogados') is the official professional association and regulatory body for lawyers in Portugal. It is a public institution that oversees the admission, registration, and discipline of lawyers. The Bar Association is responsible for upholding professional standards, promoting legal education, and protecting the interests of the legal profession and the public.

116. The Ministry of Justice ('Ministério da Justiça') is a government ministry responsible for the development and implementation of justice policies in Portugal. It oversees the functioning of the judicial system, including court administration, legal reforms, and the coordination of justice-related institutions.

117. The Attorney General's Office ('Procuradoria-Geral da República') serves as the highest judicial body for public prosecution in Portugal. It is responsible for representing the public interest, conducting criminal investigations, and overseeing public prosecutors.

118. There are also several Registration Offices (Civil,[103] Real Estate Property,[104] Commercial Companies,[105] etc.), which are government services which record and keep facts of civil life (birth, marriage, death); commercial businesses (creation of companies, board members, civil status of traders); or concerning the acquisition, transfer or encumbering of real estate property (e.g. land, houses, buildings) or movable goods subject to registration (e.g., cars, planes).

119. Notaries also play a relevant role in drafting public deeds and certifying authenticity to private documents, thereby deterring fraud in the signing of important documents such as the sale of real estate property, mortgages or wills.[106]

120. Finally, private law firms and legal organizations play a significant role in the practice of law in Portugal. These organizations are privately owned and operated, providing legal services to clients across various areas of law, such as corporate law, litigation, real estate, and more. Law firms may range in size from small boutique firms to large multinational organizations, and they employ lawyers who are members of the Bar Association.

103. The Code of Civil Registry ('Registo Civil'), enacted by Decree-Law No. 131/95 of 6 June, as last amended by Decree-Law No. 49/2018 of 14 August.
104. The Code of Real Estate Registry ('Registo Predial'), enacted by Decree-Law No. 224/84 of 6 July, as last amended by Law No. 89/2017 of 21 August.
105. Code of Commercial Registration ('Registo Comercial'), enacted by Decree-Law No. 403/86 of 3 December, as last amended by Law No. 9/2022 of 11 January.
106. The Notarial Code ('Código do Notariado'), enacted by Decree-Law No. 207/95 of 14 August, as last amended by Law No. 8/2022 of 10 January.

Chapter 3. The Bailiffs

§1. Exercise of the Profession

121. The role of a bailiff is fulfilled by enforcement agents known as 'Agentes de Execução.[107] Bailiffs, or enforcement agents, play a crucial role in the execution and enforcement of court orders, such as the collection of debts and the seizure of assets. Key regulatory issues about bailiffs in Portugal include: the notion of 'Agentes de Execução', functions and duties, authority and powers, professional regulation, and collaboration with courts and legal professionals.

122. To begin with, 'Agentes de Execução' are professionals licensed by the Chamber of Solicitors and Enforcement Agents ('Câmara dos Solicitadores e Agentes de Execução') to carry out enforcement activities. They operate as independent professionals, either as sole practitioners or as part of solicitor offices.

123. Then, Bailiffs in Portugal are responsible for executing court orders related to debt collection, asset seizure, evictions, and other enforcement actions. They ensure the enforcement of judicial decisions and the protection of the rights of both the claimant and the debtor. They have the authority to act on behalf of the court and exercise specific powers granted to them by law. They can serve legal documents, conduct property searches, seize assets, and take other necessary measures to enforce court orders.

124. Concerning supervision, the Chamber of Solicitors and Enforcement Agents regulates the profession of bailiffs in Portugal. It sets standards of professional conduct, oversees the licensing process, and addresses complaints and disciplinary matters related to enforcement agents. Bailiffs work in collaboration with courts, judges, lawyers, and other legal professionals involved in the enforcement process. They may receive instructions from courts, such as writs of execution, and work closely with the parties involved to ensure compliance with court orders.

107. Statute of Solicitors and Bailifs ('Estatuto da Ordem dos Solicitadores e dos Agentes de Execução'), enacted by Law No. 154/2015 of 14 September, as last amended by Law No. 79/2021 of 24 November.

Chapter 4. Ombudsman ('Provedor de Justiça')

125. An Ombudsman is an independent and impartial entity that handles complaints and disputes between individuals and public or private institutions. The Ombudsman investigates complaints, facilitates communication between the parties, and seeks to resolve disputes through mediation or other means.[108]

126. The Constitution of the Republic guarantees that citizens may submit complaints for actions or omissions by public authorities to the Ombudsman, who will assess them without decision-making power, directing the necessary recommendations to the competent bodies to prevent and remedy injustices, and acting independently by other means provided for in the Constitution and in the laws.[109]

127. The Ombudsman is an independent body designated by the Assembly of the Republic for a period of four years, one-time renewable for an equal period, and all public Administration bodies and agents have a special duty to cooperate with the Ombudsman in carrying out his mission.[110] The Ombudsman receives complaints from citizens concerning actions or omissions by public authorities. It has no decision-making power but may direct the necessary recommendations to the competent bodies to prevent and remedy injustices.[111]

108. *See* Ombudsman Statute ('Estatuto do Provedor de Justiça'), enacted by Law No. 9/91 of 9 April, as last amended by Law No. 17/2013 of 18 February.
109. Article 23(1) and (2) Constitution.
110. Article 23(3) and (4) Constitution.
111. Article 3 of the Ombudsman Statute ('Estatuto do Provedor de Justiça'), enacted by Law No. 9/91 of 9 April.

Part II. Jurisdiction Chapter

Chapter 1. Domestic Jurisdiction

§1. Subject Matter Jurisdiction

128. When initiating a civil lawsuit in Portugal, it is crucial to consider the jurisdictional requirements and determine the appropriate court to file the case based on the subject matter and value of the claim. The subject matter jurisdiction in civil procedure is primarily determined by the value of the claim and the nature of the case. The Portuguese legal system has different levels of courts with varying jurisdictional powers.

129. The District Court ('Tribunal Judicial de Comarca') is the Court of First Instance for most civil cases. It has subject matter jurisdiction over civil cases where the value of the claim does not exceed a certain threshold.

130. The Court of Appeals ('Tribunal da Relação') hears appeals from decisions made by the District Courts. It has subject matter jurisdiction over appeals regarding civil cases that exceed the jurisdictional threshold of the District Court.

131. The STJ ('Supremo Tribunal de Justiça') is the highest court in Portugal for civil matters. It has subject matter jurisdiction over appeals from the Court of Appeals, dealing with legal questions or cases of significant importance.

132. For purposes of appeals to the Court of Appeals and the STJ, the value of the claim has to exceed the threshold ('alçada') of the appealed court. The thresholds are EUR 5,000 for District Courts and EUR 30,000 for Court of Appeals.[112]

133. District Courts can have specialized jurisdictions, i.e., certain specialized courts have jurisdiction over specific types of civil cases (forum *ratione materiae*). Examples include the Family and Minors Courts for family law matters and the Labour Courts for employment-related disputes.[113]

112. Article 44(1) and (2) of Judicial System Organization Statute, enacted by Law No. 62/2013 of 26 August (LOSJ).
113. Article 80 of Judicial System Organization Statute (LOSJ).

134. Moreover, subject matter jurisdiction can also depend on the specific laws and regulations governing particular types of cases. For instance, cases related to intellectual property or cases related to competition and supervision have jurisdictional rules specific to courts of intellectual property and courts of competition and regulation,[114] which have enlarged or extended territorial jurisdiction. These courts have exclusive jurisdiction over cases falling within their specialized areas.[115]

§2. Venue (Territorial Jurisdiction)

135. In Portugal, the concept of venue, also known as territorial jurisdiction, determines which court has the authority to hear a civil case based on the geographic location or territorial boundaries. The Portuguese legal system follows specific rules to determine the appropriate court for a civil matter based on the defendant's domicile or the location where the dispute arose.

136. The general rule and the specific rules and criteria for determining venue in civil cases in Portugal are provided in the CPC ('Código de Processo Civil'). These rules ensure that cases are heard by the appropriate court based on the defendant's domicile or the location where the dispute arose, promoting convenience, fairness, and efficiency in the administration of justice. When initiating a civil lawsuit, it is crucial to determine the correct venue for filing the case.

137. The general rule for venue in Portugal is that the court with jurisdiction is determined based on the defendant's domicile (*forum domicilii*).[116] If the defendant is an individual, the court within whose territorial jurisdiction the defendant resides is competent to hear the case. If the defendant is a legal entity, the court within whose territorial jurisdiction the entity has its registered office or branch is competent.[117]

138. In some cases, special rules may apply to determine the venue based on the specific nature of the dispute or applicable laws. For example, in cases involving property rights or real estate disputes, jurisdiction belongs to the court within the territory where the property is located (*forum rei sitae*).[118]

139. In certain situations, the parties to a civil dispute may have the option to choose a different court within the boundaries of applicable law, the so-called choice of forum. Parties can agree to exclusive jurisdiction clauses in contracts, designating a specific court as the competent venue for resolving any disputes that may arise.[119] However, such agreements are subject to certain conditions and limitations under Portuguese law.

---

114. Article 83 of the Judicial System Organization Statute (LOSJ).
115. Article 111(1) of the Judicial System Organization Statute (LOSJ).
116. Article 71 CPC.
117. Article 81(2) CPC.
118. Article 70(1) CPC.
119. Article 94 CPC.

§3. Resolution of Jurisdiction Conflicts

140. The resolution of jurisdiction conflicts in Portuguese civil procedure law involves specific procedures and mechanisms to determine which court has the authority to hear a case when there are disputes over jurisdiction. The resolution of jurisdiction conflicts aims to ensure that cases are heard by the appropriate court, promoting legal certainty and efficient administration of justice.

141. Key aspects regarding the resolution of jurisdiction conflicts in Portugal's civil procedure law include lis pendens, declinatory exception, a central authority for jurisdiction conflicts, appellate review, and special courts and procedures.

142. To begin with, lis pendens refers to a situation where two or more courts have concurrent jurisdiction over the same dispute. In such cases, the court where the case is first filed has priority and retains jurisdiction over the case. If a subsequent case is filed in another court involving the same parties and the same cause of action, the second court must decline jurisdiction and stay the proceedings.[120]

143. Moreover, a party can raise a declinatory exception to challenge the jurisdiction of the court where the case was filed. The court will examine the grounds presented by the parties and determine if it has jurisdiction to hear the case. If the court finds that it lacks jurisdiction, it will decline to hear the case and transfer it to the appropriate court. It is considered a type of dilatory exception ('exceção dilatória'), which prevents the court from hearing the merits of the case and gives rise to the acquittal of the instance or the referral of the case to another court.[121]

144. Lack of jurisdiction can be relative or absolute. For instance, the infringement of the rules of jurisdiction on the grounds of subject matter and hierarchy and of the rules of international jurisdiction determines the absolute lack of jurisdiction of the court. It may be argued by the parties and unless it results from the violation of a private agreement of jurisdiction or preterition of a voluntary arbitral tribunal, it must be raised *ex officio* by the court as long as there is no final and unappealable judgment rendered on the substance of the cause.[122] The verification of absolute incompetence implies the acquittal of the defendant in the instance or the rejection in a preliminary order when the process allows it.[123]

145. Relative lack of jurisdiction results, for example, from the infringement of rules of jurisdiction based on the value of the case or on the judicial division of the territory.[124] It may be argued by the defendant, and in some cases, the court must *ex*

120. Articles 580 and 581 CPC.
121. Articles 576 and 577(a) CPC.
122. Article 97(1) CPC.
123. Article 99 CPC.
124. Article 102 CPC.

officio check jurisdiction on reasons, such as, for example, *forum rei sitae*, in matters concerning immovable property or the defendant's domicile concerning breach of contract.[125]

146. Conflicts of jurisdiction between Portuguese courts are solved by the STJ ('Supremo Tribunal de Justiça') or by the Court of Conflicts ('Tribunal dos Conflitos'), which will determine which court has jurisdiction in situations where there is a dispute between different courts over jurisdiction.[126] Decisions on jurisdictional conflicts may be subject to appellate review. The parties may have the right to appeal a decision on jurisdiction to a higher court. The appellate court reviews the legal reasoning and application of the law regarding the jurisdictional issue.[127]

125. Articles 103 and 104 CPC.
126. Articles 110 *et seq.* CPC.
127. Article 101 CPC.

Chapter 2. International Jurisdiction

§1. Rules Applicable in the Absence of a Treaty

147. In the absence of a treaty governing international jurisdiction, the CPC provides rules to determine the international jurisdiction of Portuguese courts in civil matters. These rules are based on the principles of proximity and effectiveness of justice and establish criteria such as the defendant's domicile, the location of property (*forum loci rei sitae*), choice of forum, and ancillary jurisdiction.

148. To begin with, Portuguese courts have international jurisdiction over a case if they have territorial jurisdiction under domestic rules.[128] According to the general rule, Portuguese courts have jurisdiction where the defendant has a domicile in Portugal. Domicile refers to the defendant's habitual residence or registered office. Regardless of the defendant's domicile, Portuguese courts may have jurisdiction where the relevant facts for the cause of action took place in the Portuguese territory (*forum loci delicti comisssi*).[129]

149. In certain cases, Portuguese courts have exclusive jurisdiction regardless of the defendant's domicile. For example, Portuguese courts have exclusive jurisdiction in matters related to real estate located in Portugal (*forum loci rei sitae*), succession to assets located in Portugal, and the validity of acts concerning Portuguese legal entities.[130] Portuguese courts have jurisdiction over cases involving rights in rem (property rights) related to assets located in Portugal. This includes disputes over ownership, possession, or other property-related matters.

150. Moreover, parties can agree in writing to confer jurisdiction on a specific Portuguese court or to waive the right to challenge the jurisdiction of a Portuguese court.[131] Such agreements are valid and enforceable, provided they meet the requirements under Portuguese law. For example, jurisdiction clauses have to be agreed or confirmed in written form.[132]

151. Finally, Portuguese courts may have jurisdiction over ancillary claims that are closely connected to a main claim that falls within their jurisdiction and which otherwise would be hard to petition or enforce.[133] This allows the court to hear related claims even if the court's jurisdiction is primarily based on another ground.

---

128. Article 62(a) CPC.
129. Article 62(b) CPC.
130. Article 63 CPC.
131. Article 94 CPC.
132. Article 94(3)(e) CPC.
133. Article 62(c) CPC.

§2. International Treaties and the EU Regulation Brussels I Recast

152. Portugal is a party to several international treaties that govern international jurisdiction in civil procedure.[134] These treaties establish rules and principles to determine which court has jurisdiction in cross-border disputes, addressing jurisdictional issues and the recognition and enforcement of judgments between the contracting parties. Some of the key treaties relevant to international jurisdiction in civil procedure in Portugal include the Brussels and Lugano Conventions[135] and the Hague Convention on Choice of Court Agreements.[136]

153. The Lugano Convention, officially known as the Convention on Jurisdiction and the Recognition and Enforcement of Judgments in Civil and Commercial Matters, is applicable to civil and commercial matters involving the EU Member States, Iceland, Norway, and Switzerland. It provides rules on jurisdiction, choice of forum, and recognition and enforcement of judgments in cross-border cases among the contracting states. Moreover, Portugal is also a party to the Hague Convention on Choice of Court Agreements. The convention establishes rules for recognizing and enforcing exclusive choice of court agreements between parties in international commercial transactions.

154. As a Member State of the EU, Portugal applies Regulation (EU) No. 1215/2012 (Brussels I recast).[137] This Regulation governs jurisdiction and the recognition and enforcement of judgments in civil and commercial matters within the EU. It establishes rules for determining the court with jurisdiction in cross-border cases involving EU Member States, including rules on choice of forum, defendant's domicile, and special jurisdictional grounds. Regulation Brussels I recast determines the courts of which Member State have jurisdiction to decide on a civil and commercial dispute where there is an international element and further provides that a judgment given in a Member State shall be recognized in the other Member States without any special procedure of enforceability being required, by means of a certificate concerning a judgment and or a certificate concerning an authentic instrument/court settlement.

155. The Regulation prevails over the provisions of the Code of civil procedure on international jurisdiction, which therefore are left with residual value only.

134. https://dgaj.justica.gov.pt/Tribunais/Cooperacao-Judiciaria-Internacional/Convencoes-regulamentos.

135. Brussels Convention on Jurisdiction and the Enforcement of Judgments in Civil and Commercial Matters, concluded on 27 Sep. 1968, and Lugano Convention on Jurisdiction and the Enforcement of Judgments in Civil and Commercial Matters, concluded on 16 Sep. 1988 between Member States and EFTA States (revised in 2007).

136. Convention of 30 Jun. 2005 on Choice of Court Agreements. Available at https://www.hcch.net/en/instruments/conventions/full-text/?cid=98.

137. Regulation (EU) No. 1215/2012 of the European Parliament and of the Council of 12 Dec. 2012 on jurisdiction and the recognition and enforcement of judgments in civil and commercial matters (replaced Regulation 44/2001).

According to the Court of Justice of the European Union (CJEU),[138] 'The Convention of 27 September 1968, which seeks to determine the jurisdiction of the courts of the contracting states in civil matters, must override national provisions which are incompatible with it.' And so do the provisions of Regulation Brussels I recast, as EU law prevails over conflicting national provisions.[139]

156. According to this Regulation, the jurisdiction is generally based on the defendant's domicile (*actor sequitur forum rei*),[140] and jurisdiction must always be available on this ground except in a few well-defined situations in which the subject matter of the litigation or the autonomy of the parties establishes a different linking factor. In addition to the defendant's domicile, the regulation provides alternative grounds of jurisdiction based on a close link between the court and the action or to facilitate the sound administration of justice, for example, in proceedings which have as their object rights in rem in immovable property (*forum loci rei sitae*). Finally, the weaker party in relation to insurance, consumer contracts and employment is protected by rules of jurisdiction more favourable to their interests, as in principle, they are able to resort to the courts of their domicile.

157. Moreover, in alternative to the defendant's domicile, Portuguese courts may have special jurisdiction over proceedings concerning persons domiciled in another Member State in special matters concerning namely a contract, if the place of performance of the obligation in question is located in Portugal,[141] as well as on matters of tort, delict or quasi-delict, if the place where the harmful event occurred or may occur is located in Portugal.[142] For instance, concerning *ubiquitous infringement* on the Internet, the mere accessibility of a website in a country may not be enough to establish jurisdiction in case the defendant does not direct his activity to that country nor engage in activities therein. According to the CJEU, 'the jurisdictional rules [are to be] interpreted in such a way as to enable a normally well-informed defendant reasonably to predict before which courts, other than those of the State in which he is domiciled, he may be sued'.[143]

---

138. Judgment of the Court (Fourth Chamber) of 15 Nov. 1983, C-288/82, *Ferdinand M.J.J. Duijnstee v. Lodewijk Goderbauer* [1983] *ECR* 03663. *See also* STJ, judgment of 3 Oct. 2007, proc. 07S922, available at www.dgsi.pt/.

139. *See* https://eur-lex.europa.eu/EN/legal-content/glossary/primacy-of-eu-law-precedence-supremacy.html.

140. Article 4(1) of Brussels I recast. Companies or other legal persons or associations of natural or legal persons are deemed to be domiciled in Portugal in case this is the place where they have their statutory seat, central administration, or principal place of business – Article 63(1). Concerning natural persons, the judge applies its internal legislation – Article 62(1). Article 82(1) of the Civil Code provides that a person has domicile at the place of his/her habitual residence.

141. Article 7(1) of Brussels I recast.

142. Article 7(2) of Brussels I recast.

143. Judgment of 17 Jun. 1992, C-26/91, *Jakob Handte & Co. GmbH v. Traitements Mécano-chimiques des Surfaces SA* [1992] *ECR* I-3967.

158. Concerning offences to personality rights perpetuated by content made available on a website, moreover, the CJEU[144] held that the victim may sue the infringer for all the damages suffered either before the courts of the Member State of establishment of the infringer or before the courts of the Member State in which the victim has his/her centre of interests, or in alternative, the victim may sue the infringer before the courts of each Member State in which a content is or has been available online but only for damages caused in the territory of each Member State.

159. Regardless of domicile, Portuguese courts have *exclusive jurisdiction* in certain matters,[145] for example, concerning the registration or validity of patents, trademarks, designs, or other similar rights required to be deposited or registered if Portugal is the Member State in which the deposit or registration has been applied for, has taken place or is under the terms of an EU instrument or an international convention deemed to have taken place.

160. Jurisdiction of Portuguese courts may also be agreed by the parties in a *choice of court* ('pacto atributivo de jurisdição'), provided that one or more of whom is or are domiciled in a Member State, to settle any disputes which have arisen or which may arise in connection with a particular legal relationship.[146] Choice of court agreements shall be produced in writing or evidenced in writing, including any communication by electronic means which provides a durable record of the agreement; or in a form which accords with practices which the parties have established between themselves; or in international trade or commerce, in a form which accords with a usage of which the parties are or ought to have been aware and which in such trade or commerce is widely known to, and regularly observed by, parties to contracts of the type involved in the particular trade or commerce concerned.[147] According to the CJEU, no other *formal requirements*, including language, can be provided under domestic law.[148]

161. Concerning intellectual property contracts, there is jurisprudence holding that a choice of court agreement for a licence contract does not include litigations on the termination of the contract and tort liability caused by unlawful acts committed by the plaintiff in Portugal.[149] However, the STJ accepts that agreements on choice of court concern any dispute that arises out of the main contract and therefore jurisdiction of the chosen court includes all issues, either contractual or tort, that result thereof.[150] The Lisbon Court of Appeal (TRL) held that the courts cannot

144. Judgment of 25 Oct. 2011, joined cases C-509/09 e C-161/10, *eDate Advertising* c. *X e Olivier e Robert Martinez* c. *MGN*.
145. Article 24 of Brussels I recast.
146. Article 25(1) of Brussels I recast.
147. Article 25(2) of Brussels I recast.
148. Judgment of 24 Jun. 1981, C-150/80, *Elefanten Schuh GmbH v. Jacqmain* [1981] *ECR 01671* ('the legislation of a contracting state may not allow the validity of such an agreement to be called in question solely on the ground that the language used is not that prescribed by that legislation.'). *See also* STJ, judgment of 8 Oct. 2009, proc. 5138/06.8TBSTS.S1, available at www.dgsi.pt/.
149. 'Supremo Tribunal de Justiça', judgment of 12 Apr. 1997, proc. 98B292, available at www.dgsi.pt/.
150. Judgment of 8 Oct. 2009, proc. 5138/06.8TBSTS.S1, available at www.dgsi.pt/.

control the grounds of jurisdiction of a court chosen by agreement.[151] Moreover, the STJ held that a party to a choice of court agreement can waive from such jurisdiction agreement in case it is provided for therein.[152] However, according to the CJEU, the court shall decline on its own motion the jurisdiction conferred to it by an unfair term.[153]

162. Portuguese courts also have jurisdiction to hear *provisional, including protective, measures* as may be available under Portuguese law, even if, under Brussels I recast, the courts of another Member State have jurisdiction as to the substance of the matter.[154] The TRL held in several judgments that an international arbitration agreement does not exclude the international jurisdiction of Portuguese courts concerning related interim provisional procedures.[155] In any case, matters such as arbitration are excluded from the scope of application of Brussels I Regulation.[156]

151. 'Tribunal da Relação de Lisboa', judgment 21 May 2009, proc. 8748/2008-6, available at www.dgsi.pt.
152. 'Supremo Tribunal de Justiça', judgment of 17 Dec. 2004, proc. 04B4076, available at www.dgsi.pt/.
153. Judgment of the Court of 27 Jun. 2000, joined cases C-240/98 to C-244/98, *Océano Grupo Editorial SA v. Roció Murciano Quintero (C-240/98)* and *Salvat Editores SA v. José M. Sánchez Alcón Prades (C-241/98), José Luis Copano Badillo (C-242/98), Mohammed Berroane (C-243/98) and Emilio Viñas Feliú (C-244/98)* [2000] *ECR* I-04941.
154. Article 31 of Brussels I recast.
155. 'Tribunal da Relação de Lisboa', judgments of 2 Dec. 2003 and of 13 Mar. 2007, available at www.dgsi.pt.
156. Article 1(2)(d) of Brussels I recast.

Part III. Actions and Claims

Chapter 1. Actions

§1. Definition of Actions

163. In Portugal's civil legal system, various actions can be brought before the courts to seek legal remedies and resolve disputes.

164. Actions, also known as lawsuits or legal proceedings, are formal legal processes initiated by one party (the plaintiff or claimant) against another party (the defendant) to seek a legal remedy or resolution of a dispute. Actions can cover a wide range of civil matters, including contract disputes, tort claims, property disputes, family law matters, and more.

165. Civil procedure is governed by the adversarial principle. The court only solves the conflict of interests that the action presupposes if the resolution has been requested by one of the parties and the other has been called to present opposition, as only in the exceptional cases provided for by law can measures be taken against a certain person without that person being previously heard.[157] The adversarial principle, as a 'structuring principle of civil proceedings and a fundamental procedural guarantee',[158] must be observed and enforced throughout the entire process. It prevents judges from deciding questions of law or fact without the parties having had the opportunity to comment on them, except in the case of manifest unnecessary need.[159]

166. In Portuguese civil procedure, there are declarative actions ('ação declarativa') and executive actions ('ação executiva').[160]

167. Declarative actions may be of simple appreciation, condemnation or constitutive, depending on their purpose: for simple assessments, obtaining only a declaration of the existence or non-existence of a right or fact (e.g., ownership of real estate property, inexistence of partnership[161]); for condemnation, demanding the

157. Article 3(1) and (2) CPC.
158. STJ judgment of 17 Dec. 2019, Case No. 363/07.7TVPRT-D.P2.S1, www.dgsi.pt.
159. Article 3(3) CPC.
160. Article 10(1) CPC.
161. *See* for example STJ judgment of 6 Jun. 2019, Case No. 639/13.4TBOAZ.P1.S1, in www.dgsi.pt.

performance of a thing or a fact (e.g., payment of the price, delivery of the good); assuming or foreseeing the violation of a right (e.g., liability for damages); and for the constitutive ones, to authorize a change in the existing legal order (e.g., termination of contract, divorce).[162]

168. Executive actions ('ação executiva') are those in which the creditor requests the appropriate measures for the coercive fulfilment of an obligation owed to him based on a title by which the purpose and limits of the executive action are determined and which may consist of the payment of a certain amount, the delivery of a certain thing or the provision of a fact, whether positive or negative.[163]

§2. Admissibility (In Special, Standing)

169. Admissibility refers to the criteria and requirements that need to be met for an action to be considered valid and acceptable by the court. One important aspect of admissibility is standing, which means that the party bringing the action must have a direct and legitimate interest in the matter at hand. The plaintiff must demonstrate that they have legal standing to bring the action and that they have suffered harm or have a legal right that has been violated.

170. Standing requires, to begin with, judicial personality ('personalidade judiciária'). The principle is that whoever has legal personality also has judicial personality,[164] which, however, is extended to other legal entities, such as laying inheritances ('herança jacente'), associations without legal personality and special commissions.[165]

171. Besides judicial personality, the parties have to be legitimate, i.e., the claimant must have a direct interest in petition and the plaintiff must have a direct interest in contesting the claim, meaning that the action may produce a benefit or harm to any of the parties, respectively.[166]

172. If the disputed material relationship concerns several persons, the respective action may be brought by all or against all interested parties, and the same applies if the law or agreement permits the right to be exercised by only one person or the common obligation to be required of only one of the interested parties – 'voluntary joinder' ('litisconsórcio voluntário').[167] However, the intervention of the various parties interested in the disputed relationship may be required by law or by agreement, and in such cases, the absence of any of them is a reason for illegitimacy; the same applies where, due to the very nature of the legal relationship, the

162. Article 10(2) and (3) CPC.
163. Article 10(4)–(6) CPC.
164. Article 11 CPC.
165. Article 12 CPC.
166. Article 30(1) and (2) CPC.
167. Article 32 CPC.

intervention of all interested parties is necessary for the decision to produce its normal useful effect, i.e., to definitively regulate the specific situation of the parties in relation to the request made, even where not binding on the other interested parties – 'necessary joinder' ('litisconsórcio necessário').[168] For example, the exercise of contractual rights of preference with several holders[169] or the exercise of inheritance rights by or against all heirs.[170]

173. In 'necessary joinder' of parties, there is a single action with a plurality of subjects; in 'voluntary joinder', there is a simple accumulation of actions, each litigant retaining a position of independence in relation to his counterparts.[171]

§3. Vexatious Litigation

174. Vexatious litigation refers to the abuse or misuse of the legal system by repeatedly initiating baseless or frivolous lawsuits, causing harassment or undue burden on the opposing party or the court. In Portugal, as in many jurisdictions, vexatious litigation is discouraged and subject to judicial scrutiny. The court may dismiss or strike out actions that are deemed vexatious or abusive, and the party responsible for such litigation may be subject to sanctions or penalties.

175. One of the principles of civil procedure is the obligation of the parties to act in good faith and to observe duties of cooperation.[172] A party found to have litigated in bad faith is sentenced to a fine and compensation to the opposing party if it so requests. A litigant is deemed in bad faith where, with intent or serious negligence, it has filed a claim or opposition whose lack of foundation should not be ignored and/or altered the truth of the facts or omitted facts relevant to the decision of the case, and/or committed a serious omission of the duty of cooperation, and/or made a manifestly reprehensible use of the process or procedural means, with the aim of achieving an illegal objective, preventing the discovery of the truth, hindering the action of justice or delaying, without serious grounds, the final and unappealable decision.[173] A party condemned for litigation in bad faith can always appeal in one level of such decision regardless of the value of the cause and the loss of suit.[174]

176. Compensation for litigation in bad faith may consist of the reimbursement of expenses that the bad faith of the litigant has forced the opposing party, including the fees of agents or technicians, as well as the satisfaction of the remaining damages suffered by the opposing party as a direct or indirect consequence of bad

168. Article 33 CPC.
169. Article 419 of the CC.
170. Article 2019 of the CC.
171. Article 35 CPC.
172. Article 8 CPC.
173. Article 542(1) and (2) CPC.
174. Article 542(3) CPC.

faith.[175] However, there is judicial discretion in fixing the compensation, as the judge chooses the compensation he deems most appropriate for the conduct of the litigant in bad faith, provided it sets it at a certain reasonable and fair amount, which can be lower than the sums of expenses and fees submitted by the other party.[176] The party's representative in court may be held liable towards the party where bad faith litigation is caused by him.[177]

175. Article 543(1) CPC
176. Article 543(2) and (3) CPC.
177. Article 545 CPC.

Chapter 2. Claims and Defences

§1. Definition of Claims

177. Claims, also known as causes of action or causes of claim, are assertions made by the plaintiff or claimant seeking a legal remedy or relief from the court. A claim is the primary request made by the plaintiff and forms the basis of the lawsuit. Examples of claims include demands for payment of a debt, requests for specific performance of a contract, or claims for damages in a tort case.

§2. Distinctions

178. There are main claims and ancillary claims. Main claims are the principal claims made by the plaintiff, which form the core of the lawsuit. They are the primary requests for relief sought by the plaintiff. Ancillary claims, also known as incidental claims or subsidiary claims, are closely related to the main claim and are considered secondary in nature. They arise from the same factual and legal basis as the main claim and are typically resolved together with the main claim.

179. As for defences, they are arguments and legal positions put forward by the defendant to challenge or counter the plaintiff's claims. Defence is called contestation ('contestação'), and it can be by *objection* ('impugnação') when the defendant contradicts the facts articulated in the petition or when he claims that these facts cannot produce the legal effect intended by the plaintiff, or *by exception*, when he argues facts that prevent the assessment of the merits of the action or that, serving as an impeding, modifying or extinguishing cause of the right invoked by the plaintiff, determine the total or partial rejection of the request.[178]

180. Defences aim to demonstrate that the plaintiff's claims lack merit or are otherwise legally flawed. Defences can include various legal arguments, such as denial of the allegations, statute of limitations, lack of jurisdiction, lack of standing, or failure to state a valid cause of action.

181. There are defences on the merits and procedural exceptions. A defence on the merits challenges the substantive validity of the plaintiff's claims. It asserts that, even if the plaintiff's allegations are accepted as true, the defendant has a valid defence against them. Procedural exceptions, also known as dilatory exceptions or preliminary objections, focus on procedural issues rather than the merits of the case. These exceptions aim to challenge the validity of the lawsuit based on procedural defects or irregularities, such as lack of jurisdiction, improper service of process, or failure to comply with procedural requirements.

178. Article 571(1) and (2) CPC.

§3. COUNTERCLAIMS

182. The defendant can also be entitled to put a counterclaim. In fact, the defendant may, in a counterclaim, bring claims against the plaintiff, which is admissible in four groups of cases. First, when it arises from the legal fact that serves as a basis for the action or defence. Second, to make effective the right to improvements or expenses related to the thing whose delivery is requested. Third, to get recognition of a claim, either to obtain compensation or to obtain payment of the amount by which the claimed claim exceeds that of the plaintiff. Fourth, to achieve, for the defendant's benefit, the same legal effect that the plaintiff intends to obtain.[179]

179. Article 266 CPC.

Chapter 3. Sanctions on Procedural Irregularities

§1. Formal Requirements

183. In Portuguese civil procedure, there are sanctions for procedural irregularities that fail to comply with formal requirements and time limits. These sanctions are aimed at promoting the efficient and orderly administration of justice.

184. To begin with, procedural rules specify certain formal requirements that parties must follow when submitting documents, presenting evidence, or fulfilling other procedural obligations. Failure to comply with these formal requirements can result in sanctions, such as the rejection of a document or the disregard of evidence. The general rule is that procedural acts have the form that, in the simplest terms, best corresponds to the purpose they aim to achieve; however, those which are to be reduced to writing must be composed in such a way as to leave no doubt about their formal authenticity and written in such a way as to make their content clear, with the abbreviations used having an unequivocal meaning.[180]

§2. Time Limits

185. Moreover, Portuguese civil procedure imposes specific time limits for performing certain procedural acts, such as filing a claim, submitting evidence, or responding to a summons. If a party fails to meet these time limits, the court may impose sanctions, such as the loss of a right or the exclusion of a late submission. For example, documents intended to prove the grounds of the action or defence must be presented with the pleading in which the corresponding facts are alleged; otherwise, they may be presented up to twenty days before the date on which the final hearing takes place, but the party is sentenced to a fine unless it proves that it was unable to offer them with the pleading; after that time limit, only documents which could not be submitted up to that moment are admitted, as well as those whose presentation has become necessary due to a later occurrence.[181]

§3. Consequences of Procedural Irregularities

186. The consequences of procedural irregularities depend on the nature and severity of the non-compliance. In some cases, the court may give the non-compliant party an opportunity to remedy the irregularity within a specified time frame. However, if the non-compliance is significant or repetitive, the court may impose more severe sanctions, such as the dismissal of a claim, exclusion of evidence, or even costs or penalties. The court has discretion in deciding whether to apply sanctions for procedural irregularities and the extent of the sanctions. The

180. Article 131(1) and (3) CPC.
181. Article 423 CPC.

court takes into account the specific circumstances of the case, the reasons for the non-compliance, and the overall interests of justice.

187. In certain specific cases, the practice of an act that the law does not admit, as well as the omission of an act or a formality that the law prescribes, produces nullity. For instance, the entire process is null and void when the initial petition is inept because, for example, the indication of the request or the reason for the request is missing or unintelligible.[182] After the initial petition, acts are null and void where the defendant has not been summoned.[183]

§4. JUDICIAL DISCRETION

188. There is, however, room for some judicial discretion. Except for cases expressly provided by law, other irregularities only produce nullity when the law declares it or when the irregularity committed may influence the examination or decision of the case,[184] which is for the court to determine. Moreover, when an act has to be annulled, the subsequent terms that absolutely depend on it are also annulled, but the nullity of a part of the act does not prejudice the other parts that are independent of it, and if the defect from which the act suffers prevents the production of a certain effect, the effects for the production of which the act proves to be suitable are not considered to be necessarily harmed.[185] This is a manifestation of the general principle of conservation of legal acts and a corollary of the principle of economy of legal acts.

182. Article 186(1) and (2)(a) CPC.
183. Article 187(1) CPC.
184. Article 195(1) CPC.
185. Article 195(2) and (3).

Part IV. Proceedings

Chapter 1. Pre-trial Proceedings

189. Pre-trial proceedings in civil procedure refer to the stage of litigation that takes place before the actual trial. During this phase, the parties involved in a civil lawsuit engage in various activities to prepare for trial and potentially resolve the dispute through settlement or alternative dispute resolution methods. The specific pre-trial proceedings can vary based on the jurisdiction and the rules of civil procedure applicable to the case.

190. The parties prepare trial documents, including witness lists, exhibit lists, and trial briefs. These documents outline the arguments, evidence, and witnesses to be presented during the trial. Similar to other legal systems, Portuguese civil procedure allows for the exchange of evidence and information through the process of discovery. Parties can request the production of documents, submit written questions ('perguntas'), and request witness statements. In complex cases, the court may appoint experts to provide specialized opinions on technical or scientific matters. The parties can present their own expert evidence as well.

191. General pre-trial proceedings in Portuguese civil procedure include petition and defence, discover and expert evidence, preliminary hearings, pre-trial conferences, settlement negotiations, and pre-trial motions.

192. The plaintiff initiates the civil lawsuit by filing a petition ('petição inicial') with the court, stating the claims and supporting facts. In the petition, the plaintiff must: (a) designate the court in which the action is filed and identify the parties, indicating notably their names, domiciles or headquarters, (b) indicate the legal representative's professional domicile, (c) the form of the process, (d) expose the essential facts that constitute the cause of action and the reasons of law that serve as a basis for the action, (e) formulate the request, (f) declare the value of the claim, and (g) appoint the enforcement agent in charge of executing the summons or the judicial representative responsible for its promotion.[186] With the presentation of the initial petition, the plaintiff must prove the payment of the court fee due or the granting of the benefit of legal aid, in the form of waiver thereof.[187]

186. Article 522(1) CPC.
187. Article 522(7) CPC.

193. The defendant then submits a response ('contestação') to the petition, addressing the allegations and presenting defences. In principle, the defendant may answer within thirty days of the court citation, and when the deadline for the defence by the various defendants ends on different days, the defence of all or each of them may be offered until the end of the deadline that started to run last.[188]

194. In the contestation, both the defence by objection ('impugnação') and by exception apply: (a) by objection when he contradicts the facts articulated in the petition or when he claims that these facts cannot produce the legal effect intended by the plaintiff; (b) by exception when alleging facts that prevent the assessment of the merits of the action or that, serving as an impeding, modifying or extinguishing cause of the right invoked by the plaintiff, determine the total or partial rejection of the request.

195. When contesting, the defendant must take a definite position on the facts that constitute the cause of action invoked by the plaintiff, as uncontested facts are considered admitted by agreement, unless they are in opposition to the defence considered a whole, if a confession about them is not admissible or if they can only be proved by a written document.[189]

196. The defendant can argue dilatory exceptions or peremptory exceptions: dilatory exceptions prevent the court from hearing the merits of the case and give rise to the acquittal of the instance or the referral of the case to another court, while peremptory exceptions imply the total or partial acquittal of the request and consist of invoking facts that prevent, modify or extinguish the legal effect of the facts articulated by the author.[190] Examples of dilatory exceptions include: (a) the lack of court jurisdiction, (b) the lack of standing of any of the parties, (c) the lack of a lawyer where required, and (d) lis pendens or res judicata.[191] In particular, the lis pendens and the res judicata exceptions presuppose the repetition of a cause, either while the previous one is still ongoing (lis pendens) or after the first cause has been decided by a sentence that no longer admits an ordinary appeal (res judicata). Bot exceptions are intended to prevent the court from contradicting or reproducing a previous decision.[192]

197. The defendant may present a counterclaim, which must be expressly identified and deduced separately in the defence, explaining the grounds and concluding the request.[193] A counterclaim is admissible if it arises from the legal fact that serves as a basis for the action or defence or to make effective the right to improvements or expenses related to the thing whose delivery is requested or to get recognition of a claim, either to obtain compensation or to obtain payment of the amount by which

188. Article 569(1) and (2) CPC.
189. Article 574(1) and (2) CPC.
190. Article 576(2) and (3) CPC.
191. Article 577 CPC.
192. Article 580 CPC.
193. Article 583 CPC.

the claimed claim exceeds that of the plaintiff, or finally, to achieve, for the defendant's benefit, the same legal effect that the plaintiff intends to obtain.[194]

198. A reply to the counterclaim is only admissible for the plaintiff to present a full defence on the subject of the counterclaim, and he cannot file a new counterclaim against it.[195]

199. In Portuguese civil procedure, a preliminary hearing ('audiência prévia') is often held to establish the points of agreement and disagreement between the parties. The judge may attempt to promote a settlement and may order the exchange of documents and evidence. It is also scheduled to organize and streamline the trial proceedings. The judge discusses the evidence, identifies key issues, determines the need for witnesses, and sets a trial date.

200. A preliminary hearing may be called for one or more of the following purposes:[196] (a) to carry out an attempt at conciliation; (b) to provide the parties with a discussion of fact and law, in cases where the judge has to decide on dilatory exceptions or when he intends to know immediately, in whole or in part, the merits of the case; (c) to discuss the positions of the parties, with a view to defining the terms of the dispute, and to correct any presentations or inaccuracies in the exposition of the facts that still exist or become patent following the debate; (d) to issue a remedial order ('despacho saneador'); (e) to determine the formal evolution, simplification or procedural agility; (f) having issued a remedial order, when the action has to proceed, the judge issues an order to identify the object of the litigation and to state the subjects of the evidence; and (g) to schedule, after hearing the representatives, the acts to be carried out at the final hearing, establish the number of sessions and their duration and designate the respective data. The absence of the parties or their representatives does not constitute a reason for postponement.[197]

201. Throughout the pre-trial phase, parties may engage in settlement negotiations to try to resolve the dispute amicably. Mediation and other alternative dispute resolution methods can also be employed to facilitate a settlement. In special, the Code of civil procedure provides the attempt at conciliation ('tentativa de conciliação'), which may take place at any stage of the proceedings when the cause falls within the powers of disposition of the parties, provided that the parties jointly request it or the judge deems it opportune.[198] The attempt at conciliation is presided over by the judge, who must actively strive to obtain the most appropriate equity solution for the terms of the dispute.[199]

202. Parties may file pre-trial motions ('incidentes processuais') to address specific legal issues before the trial. These motions may relate to the admissibility of

194. Article 266 CPC.
195. Article 584 CPC
196. Article 591(1) CPC.
197. Article 591(3) CPC.
198. Article 594(1) CPC.
199. Article 594(3) CPC.

evidence, clarification of points of law, or other procedural matters. For example, in third-party embargoes, a third party who is not a party to the cause and has the possession or any right incompatible with the performance or scope of a pledge or any act of seizure or delivery of assets ordered by the court is entitled to enforce his or her right or possession deducting third-party embargoes against the action.[200]

203. If it is presented in time and there are no other reasons for the immediate rejection of the motion for embargo, the necessary evidentiary steps are taken, and the embargo is received or rejected depending on whether or not there is a serious probability of the existence of the right invoked by the appellant.[201]

200. Article 342 CPC.
201. Article 345 CPC.

Chapter 2. Proceedings in First Instance

§1. Adversarial Proceedings

I. Ordinary Proceedings

A. *Introduction of the Claim*

204. In Portuguese civil procedure, proceedings in the first instance generally follow the adversarial and ordinary process. The steps involved in the ordinary proceedings concern, in particular, the introduction of the claim, the notice, and the summary judgment.

205. The plaintiff initiates the civil lawsuit by filing a written complaint ('petição inicial') with the competent court. The complaint should include the necessary information, such as the parties' identification, a clear statement of the facts, the legal grounds for the claim, and the specific requests for relief. Once the complaint is filed, the court ensures that the defendant is properly notified ('citação') of the lawsuit. This involves serving a copy of the complaint and related documents to the defendant, informing them of the nature of the claim and the court where the case is pending.

206. In certain cases, the Portuguese civil procedure allows for summary judgment to be rendered without a full trial. Summary judgment may be granted if the court finds that there is no genuine dispute of material facts and that the law is clear and favours one party. This can lead to an early resolution of the case before a full trial.[202]

B. *Progress of Proceedings*

207. The progress of proceedings in the first instance generally includes the following stages and elements: introductory hearing and case management (e.g., determination of the trial date and the calendar for the exchange of trial briefs), preliminary measures (including production of documents), purely written procedure, trial (including representation of parties, examination by the trial judge, adjournment), and opinion by the 'ministère public'.

208. Depending on the complexity of the case and the court's discretion, an introductory hearing ('audiência preliminar') may be scheduled.[203] This hearing serves as a case management tool, allowing the court to discuss the issues, define

202. Article 567(3) CPC. *See* STJ judgment of 26 Feb. 2019, Case No. 462/13.6TBPTL.G2.S1, www.dgsi.pt.
203. Article 591 CPC.

the scope of the dispute, and determine the trial date. During the hearing, the court may also establish the calendar for the exchange of trial briefs and other procedural deadlines.

209. Indeed, a preliminary hearing ('audiência prévia') is often held to establish the points of agreement and disagreement between the parties. The judge may attempt to promote a settlement and may order the exchange of documents and evidence. It is also scheduled to organize and streamline the trial proceedings. The judge discusses the evidence, identifies key issues, determines the need for witnesses, and sets a trial date.

210. A preliminary hearing may be called for one or more of the following purposes:[204] (a) to carry out an attempt at conciliation; (b) to provide the parties with a discussion of fact and law, in cases where the judge has to decide on dilatory exceptions or when he intends to know immediately, in whole or in part, the merits of the case; (c) to discuss the positions of the parties, with a view to defining the terms of the dispute, and to correct any presentations or inaccuracies in the exposition of the facts that still exist or become patent following the debate; (d) to issue a remedial order ('despacho saneador'); (e) to determine the formal evolution, simplification or procedural agility; (f) having issued a remedial order, when the action has to proceed, the judge issues an order to identify the object of the litigation and to state the subjects of the evidence; and (g) to schedule, after hearing the representatives, the acts to be carried out at the final hearing, establish the number of sessions and their duration and designate the respective data. The absence of the parties or their representatives does not constitute a reason for postponement.[205]

211. Before the trial, the court may order preliminary measures ('providências cautelares') to protect the rights and interests of the parties involved.[206] These measures can include the production of documents, preservation of evidence, injunctions, or other necessary actions to prevent potential harm or maintain the status quo.

212. The trial is a crucial stage of the proceedings. It involves the presentation of arguments, evidence, and examination of witnesses. The key elements of the trial process in Portuguese civil procedure include the representation of parties, examination by the trial judge, adjournment, and opinion by the 'Ministério Público'.

213. The parties are typically represented by their lawyers, who advocate for their interests during the trial. The trial judge examines the parties, witnesses, and experts, allowing them to present their testimonies, answer questions, and provide clarifications. In some cases, the trial may be adjourned ('suspensão') to allow for additional evidence or arguments to be presented or to accommodate scheduling

204. Article 591(1) CPC.
205. Article 591(3) CPC.
206. Articles 362 *et seq.* CPC.

conflicts or unforeseen circumstances, for example, when one of the parties dies or becomes extinguished, or when the court orders the suspension or there is an agreement between the parties.[207]

214. Finally, in certain types of cases, such as those involving public interests or certain family matters, the 'Ministério Público' (public prosecutor) may be involved. The 'Ministério Público' can provide an opinion (parecer) on the legal issues and the best interests of society or specific individuals.[208]

C. Judgment

215. The process of rendering a judgment in civil procedure involves several steps and considerations, including deliberation, forms, formal aspects, notice, *res judicata*, interpretation and rectification, and penalty in case of non-compliance. After the trial or the conclusion of the proceedings, the court will deliberate on the evidence, arguments, and legal issues presented. The judges involved will discuss and consider the relevant factors before reaching a decision.[209]

216. In Portuguese civil procedure, judgments can take various forms, including final judgments ('sentenças'), interlocutory judgments, or default judgments. A final judgment is a definitive decision that settles the dispute between the parties and usually concludes the proceedings in the first instance. An interlocutory judgment ('decisão interlocutória') is a partial or provisional decision that addresses specific issues during the course of the proceedings. It may relate to procedural matters, evidence, or other preliminary aspects of the case. Default judgments may be rendered if one party fails to appear or defend their interests in court after proper notice and summons.

217. The judgment should be properly drafted and include essential elements, such as the identification of the court, the parties involved, a clear statement of the decision, the reasoning behind the decision, and the legal basis supporting it.[210] After the judgment is rendered, it must be properly served to the parties involved. The parties are given notice ('citação') of the judgment so that they are informed about the decision, its content, and its implications.

218. Once a judgment becomes final and binding, it has the force of *res judicata*. This means that the issues decided in the judgment cannot be re-litigated between the same parties in subsequent proceedings. Res judicata ensures the finality and certainty of the judicial decisions.[211]

207. Articles 269 *et seq.* CPC.
208. See e.g. Articles 24 and 325 CPC.
209. Articles 605 *et seq.* CPC.
210. Article 607 CPC.
211. Articles 619 *et seq.* CPC.

219. If there are doubts or ambiguities regarding the meaning or content of a judgment, under the former Code of civil procedure, the parties could request its interpretation or rectification ('aclaração'). The Court would consider such requests and could issue clarifications or corrections if necessary.[212] The new Code in force has discontinued this special motion, but nonetheless, ambiguity or obscurity of the sentence may cause nullity of the judgment for reasons of unintelligibility.[213]

220. In some cases, if a party fails to comply with the judgment, the court may impose penalties or enforcement measures. These penalties can include fines, injunctions, or other measures aimed at ensuring compliance with the judgment.[214]

II. Provisional Proceedings

221. Provisional proceedings in Portuguese civil procedure refer to the set of legal mechanisms available to parties in order to obtain temporary relief or protection while the main lawsuit is pending. These provisional measures aim to prevent irreparable harm, preserve assets, or ensure the effectiveness of the final judgment.

222. Provisional proceedings provide temporary relief and protection before and while the main lawsuit is filed or ongoing. Some common types of provisional proceedings in civil procedure include temporary injunction ('providência cautelar'), seizure ('arresto'), anticipated production of evidence ('produção antecipada de prova'), or precautionary sale (venda antecipada').

223. A temporary injunction is a provisional measure aimed at preserving rights or preventing imminent harm before a final judgment is rendered. It may be granted when there is a well-founded fear that delay would cause irreparable damage. The court can order specific actions or prohibit certain behaviours until the main lawsuit is resolved.

224. Seizure is a provisional measure that allows a party to seize or freeze the assets of the opposing party to secure a future claim or judgment. It ensures that the assets will be available to satisfy the eventual judgment. Seizure may be granted when there is a risk of the opposing party disposing of its assets or transferring them to avoid payment.

225. In certain situations, it may be necessary to preserve or obtain evidence before the main lawsuit is initiated. The production of evidence allows a party to

212. Article 669(a) CPC of 1961.

213. Article 615(1)(c) CPC. *See* STJ judgment of 25 Nov. 2020, case No. 3283/18.6T8MTS.P1-A.S1, www.dgsi.pt. Concerning lack of reasoning, it is understood that only the total absence of factual and legal foundations causes nullity, whereas deficient, mediocre or erroneous reasoning may affect the doctrinal value of the sentence, subjecting it to the risk of being revoked or altered on appeal, but does not by itself produce nullity – vd. STJ judgment of 20 Nov. 2019, case No. 1585/12.4 TBGDM.P1.S1, www.dgsi.pt.

214. *See* e.g. Article 626(5) or 868(2) CPC.

request the collection of evidence in advance, ensuring that it is preserved for use in subsequent proceedings. In cases where the asset subject to the dispute is perishable or could significantly decrease in value over time, a party may request a precautionary sale. The court can authorize the sale of the asset and hold the proceeds until the final judgment is reached. Finally, in situations where there is a need to protect and manage assets during the litigation process, the court may appoint a temporary receiver to safeguard and administer the assets until a final decision is made.

226. Under Portuguese civil procedure law, provisional proceedings can be unspecified or specified. Specified provisional measures include measures such as temporary restitution of possession ('restituição provisória da posse'), suspension of corporate resolutions, provisional alimony, temporary reparation arbitration, seizure ('arresto'), embargo of new work, and inventory of assets ('arrolamento').[215] The CPC provides specific provisions for each of these specified provisional measures.

227. Unspecified provisional adequate measures, either conservatory or anticipatory, can be requested whenever someone shows a well-founded fear that someone else will cause serious damage to their right that is difficult to repair in order to ensure the effectiveness of the threatened right.[216]

228. Provisional proceedings are urgent. For instance, proceedings must be decided, in the first instance, within a maximum period of two months or, if the defendant has not been summoned, within fifteen days.[217] Moreover, provisional measures are instrumental to the main proceedings.[218] The basic rule is that, in any case, neither the judgment of the facts, nor the final decision rendered in the precautionary procedure have any influence on the judgment of the main action.[219]

229. With the petition, the applicant offers summary proof of the threatened right and justifies the fear of injury.[220] The adversarial principle also applies, as the court hears the respondent, except when the hearing would seriously jeopardize the purpose or effectiveness of the remedy.[221]

230. The measure is decreed as long as there is a serious probability of the existence of the right and the fear of its injury is sufficiently founded, but it may be refused by the court by reasons of proportionality, i.e., when the damage resulting from the provisional measure for the defendant considerably exceeds the damage

215. Articles 377 to 409 CPC. *See* STJ judgment of STJ 13/10/1993, case No. 084223, in www.dgsi.pt.
216. Article 362(1) CPC.
217. Article 363(1) and (2) CPC.
218. Article 364 CPC.
219. Article 364(4) CPC.
220. Article 365(1) CPC.
221. Article 366(1) CPC.

that the applicant intends to avoid with it.[222] Moreover, at the request of the defendant, the measure enacted may be replaced by adequate security whenever the security offered, after hearing the applicant, proves to be sufficient to prevent the injury or repair it in full.[223]

231. Provisional procedures are instrumental to the main proceedings. They are extinguished and, when decreed, the injunctions expire if, for instance, the applicant does not propose the action on which the measure depends within thirty days from the date on which the final and unappealable decision was notified, or, after filing the action, the process is stopped for more than thirty days, due to negligence of the applicant.[224]

232. Despite provisional measures are instrumental to the main proceedings, for reasons of procedural economy, the judge, upon application, in the same decision that enacts the measure, may exempt the applicant from the burden of bringing the main action if the matter acquired in the procedure allows him to form a secure conviction about the existence of the safeguarded right and if the nature of the measure enacted is adequate to carry out the definitive settlement of the dispute.[225]

233. Moreover, the decision rejecting the reversal of the litigation cannot be appealed from, and in principle, there is no appeal to the STJ against decisions handed down in precautionary proceedings, including those which determine the reversal of the litigation, except where it is always admissible[226] – i.e., when there is a violation of the rules of absolute jurisdiction, offence of res judicata, decision regarding the value of the case, on the grounds that it exceeds the jurisdiction of the appealed court, decision given against the standardized jurisprudence of the STJ and contradiction of judgments.[227]

234. Procedural economy also justifies that, as soon as the decision that decreed the precautionary measure and reversed the litigation becomes final, the defendant is notified, with the warning that, if he so wishes, he must file an action to challenge the existence of the protected right within thirty days following the notification, under penalty of the decreed measure being consolidated as the final composition of the dispute.[228] In other words, the provisional measure becomes the final decision.

235. Notwithstanding, the adversary subsequent to the decree of the injunction is guaranteed as, when the defendant has not been heard before the measure is

222. Article 368(1) and (2) CPC.
223. Article 368(3) CPC.
224. Article 373(1)(a) and (b) CPC.
225. Article 369(1) CPC ('inversão do contencioso').
226. Article 370(1) and (2) CPC.
227. Article 629(2) CPC. *See* STJ judgment of 7 Jun. 2018, Case No. 2877/11.5TBPDL-D.L2.S1, in www.dgsi.pt.
228. Article 371(1) CPC.

decreed, he is entitled to appeal in general terms, for example, from the order that decreed it, when it understands that, in view of the elements established, it should not have been granted.[229]

236. If the measure is considered unjustified or expires due to a fact attributable to the applicant, the latter is responsible for damages culpably caused to the defendant when he has not acted with due diligence of normal prudence.[230]

§2. DEFAULT PROCEEDINGS

237. In Portuguese civil procedure, default proceedings refer to a situation where one of the parties fails to appear or defend their interests in court after proper notice and summons. Default proceedings allow the court to continue with the case and render a judgment based on the available evidence and arguments from the appearing party. Default proceedings are not desirable or recommended for the proper administration of justice. The system generally prefers that both parties actively participate in the litigation process. However, default proceedings are available to ensure the progress of the case when one party fails to comply with their obligations to appear or defend their interests.

238. The party initiating the lawsuit (plaintiff) must ensure that the other party (defendant) is properly notified ('citação') of the lawsuit. This includes serving a copy of the complaint and related documents, along with a summons to appear in court. The notice should provide sufficient time for the defendant to respond to the lawsuit.

239. If the defendant fails to appear in court or file a defence within the specified time after being properly notified, the court may proceed with default proceedings, considering the evidence and arguments presented by the party who appeared (usually the plaintiff).

240. The court may rely on the available evidence, including documents and witness statements, to make a decision. After evaluating the evidence and arguments, the court will render a default judgment. The judgment is based on the evidence presented by the appearing party and may be in favour of the plaintiff, granting the relief sought in the lawsuit.

241. The defaulting party has the opportunity to request the setting aside of the default judgment if they can show a legitimate reason for their failure to appear or defend their interests. This request must be made within a specified timeframe and provide valid grounds for reconsideration.

229. Article 372(1)(a) CPC.
230. Article 374(1) CPC.

§3. Ex Parte Proceedings

242. Ex parte proceedings ('procedimento ex parte') refer to legal proceedings where only one party is involved, and the other party is not given an opportunity to participate or present their case. Ex parte proceedings are exceptional and generally occur in limited circumstances. In fact, ex parte proceedings are exceptional and should only be used when circumstances warrant immediate action and notice to the other party would undermine the purpose of the proceedings. The specific procedures and requirements for ex parte proceedings may vary depending on the nature of the case and the court involved. In the field of intellectual property, either patents, models and designs and marks, or copyright and related rights, there are statutory provisions concerning *inaudita altera pars* proceedings.[231]

243. Ex parte proceedings typically arise in emergency situations where immediate action is required to prevent irreparable harm or protect the interests of one party. These situations may involve urgent matters such as injunctions or temporary restraining orders.

244. In ex parte proceedings, the court may grant relief without giving prior notice to the opposing party. This is because the urgency of the situation necessitates immediate action, and providing notice to the other party may delay the process and defeat the purpose of the proceedings.

245. Ex parte proceedings often result in the granting of temporary measures ('medidas provisórias') to provide immediate relief until a full hearing can take place with the participation of both parties. These measures are temporary in nature and are subject to review and modification during subsequent proceedings where the other party can present their case.

246. Although ex parte proceedings allow for quick action to be taken, they are subject to certain limitations and safeguards to protect the rights of the absent party. The court must carefully consider the necessity and proportionality of the requested relief and ensure that the absent party's interests are not unfairly prejudiced.

247. Following ex parte proceedings, the court will typically schedule a subsequent hearing where the absent party can be heard and present their case. This ensures that the absent party has an opportunity to challenge the temporary measures and provide their perspective on the matter.

---

231. The Industrial Property Code ('Código da Propriedade Industrial'), enacted by Decree-Law No. 110/2018 of 10 December, and the Code of Copyright and Related Rights, enacted by Decree-Law No. 63/85 of 14 March (as last amended by Decree-Law No. 47/2023 of de 19 June), implementing Directive 2004/48/EC of the European Parliament and of the Councill, of 29 Apr. 2004 on the enforcement of intellectual property rights.

Chapter 3. Review Proceedings

248. Review proceedings ('recurso') provide mechanisms for the parties to challenge or seek a review of judicial decisions. These proceedings allow for the review of judgments rendered in lower courts and aim to ensure the accuracy and fairness of the decisions. Review proceedings provide a means for parties to seek a review of judgments and ensure the proper application of the law. Specific rules and requirements govern each type of review proceeding, including deadlines for filing the appeals and the grounds on which they can be based.

249. In Portuguese civil procedure law, review proceedings may be 'ordinary' or 'extraordinary'.[232] Ordinary review proceedings include appeal ('apelação') and cassation ('revista'). Extraordinary appeals include standardization of jurisprudence ('uniformação de jurisprudência') and revision of judgment ('revisão').

250. To begin with, the appeal is the most common form of review proceeding in Portuguese civil law. It allows the parties to challenge a judgment rendered by a lower court (usually a Court of First Instance) and seek its modification or reversal. The appeal is filed with a higher court, typically the Court of Appeal ('Tribunal da Relação'), which reviews the case based on the arguments presented by the parties and the evidence on record.[233]

251. Review appeal or 'cassation' ('recurso de revista') is a specific type of review proceeding available in certain cases. It allows the parties to challenge a judgment from a Court of Appeal and seek its annulment based on specific grounds, such as a violation of law or a significant procedural error. The STJ ('Supremo Tribunal de Justiça') has jurisdiction to hear cassation appeals.[234]

252. Extraordinary Appeals ('recursos extraordinários') are additional review proceedings available in exceptional circumstances. These appeals are not concerned with the review of the facts of the case but rather focus on questions of law. They allow parties to challenge decisions of the Court of Appeal based on a violation of law or a significant legal question. They are divided into review for standardization of jurisprudence ('uniformação de jurisprudência') and review for revision of judgment ('revisão').

253. Revision of judgment may be brought before the STJ on the basis of, for example, a violation of substantive law, which may consist either of an error of interpretation or application, or an error in determining the applicable rule, as well as violation or wrong application of the law of procedure.[235]

232. Article 627(2) CPC.
233. *See* Articles 644 *et seq.* CPC. According to the STJ judgment of 29 Mar. 2022, case No. 893/19.8T8BJA.E1.S1, in www.dgsi.pt, in appeals where the facts are contested the Court of Appeal is not prevented from changing the decision about the facts.
234. Articles 671 *et seq.* CPC.
235. Article 674(1) CPC.

254. Review for standardization of jurisprudence may be brought before the full civil chambers of the STJ, where this Court issues a judgment that is in contradiction with another previously issued by the same Court in the field of the same legislation and on the same fundamental question of law.[236] The Court will not admit the appeal if the orientation adopted in the appealed judgment is in accordance with the already standardized jurisprudence of thc STJ.[237]

236. Article 688(1) CPC.
237. Article 688(1) CPC.

Part V. Incidents

255. There are various incidents that can arise during the course of a civil lawsuit. These incidents involve specific actions or motions that parties can take to address specific issues or situations. Here are three common incidents in civil procedure.

§1. Interlocutory Applications

256. Interlocutory Applications ('incidentes') refer to procedural motions or applications filed by parties during the course of litigation to address specific matters or seek specific orders from the court. These applications can include requests for provisional measures, production of evidence, amendment of pleadings, appointment of experts, or any other procedural issue that arises during the proceedings. The court considers these applications and makes a decision based on the merits of the request and the applicable legal provisions.

§2. Withdrawal and Discontinuance of Action

257. A party in a civil lawsuit has the option to voluntarily withdraw or discontinue their action at any stage of the proceedings.[238] There is an important distinction to be made: whereas the withdrawal of the request ('desistência do pedido') extinguishes the right that was intended to be enforced, the withdrawal of the instance ('desistência da instância') only causes the process that had been initiated to cease.[239]

258. Withdrawal typically occurs before a final judgment is rendered, and it entails the party abandoning their claims against the opposing party. Discontinuance, however, occurs after the proceedings have commenced but before a final judgment is reached. The party who withdraws or discontinues their action may be subject to certain legal consequences, such as bearing the costs of the proceedings

238. Article 283 CPC ('liberdade de desistência, confissão ou transação').
239. Article 285 CPC.

or potentially losing the right to refile the claim. The withdrawal has to be done in writing and cannot take place where rights which the parties cannot dispose of are at stake.[240]

§3. Challenge of Judges

259. In certain circumstances, a party may have grounds to challenge the impartiality or suitability of a judge assigned to the case. This challenge is known as 'recusa de juízes' and can be made if there is a reasonable doubt about the judge's impartiality or if there are specific legal grounds for challenging the judge's competence. The challenge is typically made by submitting a motion supported by relevant facts and legal arguments.

260. Moreover, the judge may request to be excused from intervening in the case when, due to weighty circumstances, he understands that his impartiality may be suspected, for example, when: (a) there are close family ties between the judge or his/her spouse and any of the parties or person who has, in relation to the object of the cause, an interest that would allow him to be a main party in it; or (b) the judge or his/her spouse, or any relative or affine of any of them in a direct line, is a creditor or debtor of one of the parties, or has a legal interest in the decision of the lawsuit being favourable to one of the parties; or (c) the judge has received donations before or after the initiation of the proceedings or there is serious enmity or great intimacy between the judge and any of the parties or their representatives.[241]

261. The CPC provides a number of cases which justify the judge's impeachment, for example, when the judge: (a) is a party to the case, by himself (or close relatives) or as a representative of another person, or when he has an interest in it that would allow him to be a main party; or (b) has intervened in the case as a representative or expert or when there is a need to decide on an issue on which he has given an opinion or has pronounced himself, even if orally; or (c) when the person who filed a civil action against him for compensation for damages is a party to the case, or who brought a criminal charge against him, as a result of acts committed in the exercise of his duties or because of them; or (d) has witnessed or has to witness.[242] When any of these causes are verified, the judge must declare himself impeded, and the parties may request the declaration of the impediment until the sentence is handed down.[243]

262. A higher court will review the challenge and make a decision on whether to accept or reject it, either assigning a different judge or dismissing the challenge.[244]

---

240. Articles 289(1) and 290 CPC.
241. Article 120(1) CPC.
242. Article 115(1) CPC.
243. Article 116 CPC.
244. Articles 122 to 124 CPC.

Part VI. Legal Aid and Legal Costs

Chapter 1. Legal Aid

263. Legal aid ('apoio judiciário') is a system that provides financial assistance to individuals who are unable to afford the costs of legal representation and other expenses related to their legal proceedings. Legal aid aims to ensure equal access to justice and help individuals exercise their rights effectively. The constitutional right of access to law and to effective court protection is guaranteed to everyone regardless of the economic situation.[245]

264. Legal aid is governed by a specific Act,[246] and key points regarding legal aid in Portuguese civil procedure include eligibility, types of legal aid, application procedure, assessment of eligibility, legal aid certificate, choice of lawyer, and reassessment of eligibility.

265. To be eligible for legal aid, individuals must meet certain financial criteria. Legal aid is provided to natural persons (or non-profit entities) who demonstrate that they are in a situation of economic insufficiency,[247] which is assessed according to criteria based upon factors such as income, assets, and family composition.[248] The specific thresholds and requirements for eligibility may vary based on the type of legal aid being sought. Victims of domestic violence are presumed to be in situation of economic insufficiency.[249]

266. There are different types of legal aid available in Portuguese law, including full legal aid ('apoio judiciário total') and partial legal aid ('apoio judiciário parcial'). Full legal aid covers all legal costs, including lawyer's fees and court fees. Partial legal aid covers a portion of the costs, and the applicant is responsible for paying the remaining expenses.

245. Article 20(1) of the Constitution.
246. Law No. 34/2004 of 29 July, which amends the regime of access to the law and courts and implements to the national legal order Council Directive 2002/8/EC of 27 Jan. 2003 to improve access to justice in cross-border disputes by establishing minimum common rules relating to legal aid for such disputes.
247. Article 7 of Law No. 34/2004.
248. Article 8 and 8-A of Law No. 34/2004.
249. Article 8-C of Law No. 34/2004.

267. Legal aid comprises the following modalities: (a) waiver of court fees and other costs with the process; (b) appointment and payment of patron's compensation; (c) payment of the compensation of the public defender; (d) phased payment of court fees and other costs with the process; (e) appointment and phased payment of employer compensation; (f) phased payment of the compensation of the public defender; (g) assignment of enforcement agent.[250]

268. Individuals seeking legal aid must submit an application to the competent entity responsible for assessing and granting legal aid. The application should include relevant financial information and supporting documentation to demonstrate the applicant's financial need.[251] The competent entity will evaluate the application and determine whether the applicant meets the financial criteria for legal aid. The assessment takes into account the applicant's income, assets, expenses, and other relevant factors.[252]

269. Individuals receiving legal aid also have the right to a lawyer to be appointed by the Bar.[253] The lawyer's fees are paid by the legal aid system, either in full or partially, depending on the type of legal aid granted.

270. In some cases, the recipient's financial situation may change during the course of the legal proceedings. In such situations, the legal aid beneficiary may need to undergo a reassessment of their eligibility and have it cancelled.[254]

250. Article 16 of Law No. 34/2004.
251. Article 18 of Law No. 34/2004.
252. Article 20 of Law No. 34/2004
253. Article 30 of Law No. 34/2004
254. Articles 10 and 13 of Law No. 34/2004

Chapter 2. Legal Costs

271. Legal costs ('custas judiciais') refer to the expenses associated with the legal proceedings, including court fees, attorney fees, and other related expenses. These costs are generally borne by the parties involved in the litigation and are regulated by specific rules and guidelines.

272. When initiating a civil lawsuit or filing specific procedural motions, parties are required to pay court fees. The amount of court fees depends on various factors, such as the type of claim, the value of the dispute, and the stage of the proceedings. The applicable court fees are determined by legislation and subject to periodic updates.

273. Parties engaging legal representation in civil proceedings are responsible for paying attorney fees. The fees charged by lawyers can vary based on factors such as the complexity of the case, the time and effort involved, and the lawyer's experience and reputation. Attorney fees are generally negotiated between the client and the lawyer, and parties have the right to choose their legal representation.

274. Individuals who meet certain financial criteria and are unable to afford legal costs may be eligible for legal aid. Legal aid covers the costs of legal representation, including attorney fees and court fees, either in full or partially, depending on the type of legal aid granted.[255]

275. Concerning cost allocation, the general rule is that the losing party bears the legal costs of the proceedings. This includes reimbursing the winning party for their reasonable and necessary expenses, such as attorney fees and court fees. However, the court has the discretion to adjust the allocation of costs based on the circumstances of the case, including the parties' behaviour during the litigation.

276. Legal costs are governed by the Code of Civil procedure[256] and the regulation of legal costs.[257] Legal (procedural) costs include court fees, charges and party costs.[258]

277. Court fees ('taxas de justiça') correspond to the amount due for the procedural impulse of each intervener and are fixed according to the value and complexity of the cause under the terms of the regulation of legal costs.[259] By reasoned decision of the judge, a penalty court fee may be exceptionally applied when the

255. According to the STJ judgment no. 1/2022 of 10 Nov. 2021, case No. 1118/16.3T8VRL-B.G1.S1-A, DR-1/2022, of uniformization of jurisprudence, the right to request exemption from payment of court fees, referred to in para. 7 of Article 6 of the Procedural Costs Regulation, takes place with the final decision of the case becoming final.
256. Articles 527 *et seq.* CPC
257. Enacted by Decree-Law No. 34/2008, of 26 February, as last amended by Law No. 9/2022 of 11 January.
258. Article 529(1), (2), (3) and (4) CPC.
259. *See* Article 530 CPC.

action, opposition, request, appeal, claim or incident is manifestly unfounded, and the party has not acted with prudence or due diligence.[260]

278. Procedural charges ('encargos') include all expenses resulting from the conduct of the process required by the parties or ordered by the judge of the cause.[261] The judge may rule that only the requesting party bears the costs if they are manifestly unnecessary and or dilatory steps.[262]

279. Party costs include what each party has spent on the process and is entitled to be compensated by virtue of the conviction of the opposing party under the terms of the regulation of legal costs.[263]

280. Legal costs may be borne by one or both parties. The general rule provides that the decision on the action or any of its incidents or appeals condemns the party that gave rise to them (legal costs) or, where the action was not successful, who took advantage of the process, and it is understood that the unsuccessful party gives cause at the costs of the process, in the proportion in which it is unsuccessful.[264]

260. Article 531 CPC.
261. Article 532 CPC.
262. Article 532(4) and (5) CPC.
263. Article 533 CPC.
264. Article 527(1) and (2) CPC.

Part VII. Evidence

Chapter 1. Burden of Proof

281. The rules regarding evidence aim to ensure the fair and effective presentation of facts in a civil lawsuit. Evidence rules (*ius probandi*) are provided by the CPC and also by the CC.

282. Evidence has the function of demonstrating the reality of facts.[265] The basic is that it is up to the person who invokes a right to prove the constitutive facts of the alleged right and to the person against whom the invocation is made the proof of impeding, modifying or extinguishing facts of the invoked right.[266] The burden of proof is different for special cases, for example, where the right invoked by the author is subject to a suspensive condition or an initial term because it is up to him to prove that the condition was verified or the term expired; if the right is subject to a resolutive condition or a final term, it is up to the defendant to prove the verification of the condition or the expiration of the term.[267]

283. The burden of proof can by reversed by legal presumption, waiver or release, or valid agreement, and, in general, whenever so determined by the law, notably when the opposing party, with fault, made it impossible for the burdened party to prove it.[268] Agreements that reverse the burden of proof are allowed except if the right is unavailable to the parties or the reversal makes it excessively difficult for one of them to exercise the right, and the same applies to any convention that excludes some legal means of proof or admits a different means of proof from the legal ones or, in any case, if the proof rule is determined by reasons of public policy.[269]

284. The instruction ('instrução') concerns the topics or facts which require evidence.[270] Under the inquisitorial principle, the judge must carry out or order, even *ex officio*, all the steps necessary to ascertain the truth and the fair composition of the dispute regarding the facts that it is lawful for him to know.[271] Some facts do

265. Article 341 of the CC.
266. Article 341(1) and (2) of the CC.
267. Article 343(3) of the CC.
268. Article 344(1) and (2) of the CC.
269. Article 345 of the CC.
270. Article 410 CPC.
271. Article 411 CPC.

not require allegation or proof, such as well-known or generally known facts, as well as facts that the court is aware of by virtue of the exercise of its functions.[272]

285. In principle, all evidence produced must be taken into account by the court.[273] In case of doubt about the reality of a fact and about which party bears the burden of proof, the court decides against the party who benefits from the fact.[274] The burden of proof refers to the responsibility of each party to prove the facts they rely on to support their claims or defences. In general, the party who asserts a certain fact has the burden of proving it. The standard of proof required is the preponderance of evidence, which means that the facts must be more likely than not to be true.

286. The party who asserts a certain fact has the burden of proving it. It is the responsibility of the party to present admissible evidence to support their claims or defences. Failure to present sufficient evidence may result in the court ruling against that party on the specific issue.

272. Article 412 CPC.
273. Article 413 CPC.
274. Article 414 CPC.

Chapter 2. Admissibility of Evidence

287. The Civil Code provides the following types of evidence: confession,[275] documentary evidence (private documents, notarized documents, public deeds, etc.),[276] expert evidence,[277] court inspection,[278] and witnessing.[279] The admissibility of each type of evidence is governed by specific requirements and criteria. Not all evidence is automatically admissible in civil procedure, as it is subject to certain rules and requirements. The court will assess whether the evidence is relevant, lawful, and obtained in a manner consistent with the principles of fairness and due process.

288. On one hand, the evidence must be relevant to the issues in dispute. It should have a logical connection to the facts at issue and be capable of shedding light on the matters to be decided by the court. On the other hand, the evidence must be obtained in a lawful manner. This means that it should not be obtained through illegal or unethical means, such as through the violation of privacy rights or the use of coercion. Under the adversarial hearing principle, evidence shall not be admitted or produced without a contradictory hearing by the party to whom it must be opposed, who has the right to intervene in all acts of preparation and production of evidence as well as to challenge both the admission and the probative value of pre-constituted evidence.[280]

289. Moreover, not only the parties but also all other participants in the proceedings have an obligation of cooperation, according to which, when conducting and intervening in the process, magistrates, legal representatives and the parties themselves must cooperate with each other, contributing to obtain, with brevity and efficiency, the fair composition of the dispute.[281] In special, the judge may, at any time during the proceedings, hear the parties, their representatives or legal representatives, inviting them to provide clarifications on matters of fact or law that appear to be relevant and informing the other party of the due diligence results, those persons are obliged to appear whenever they are notified to do so and, in principle, to provide the clarifications requested of them.[282]

290. In particular, upon the parties lies a duty of procedural good faith because they must act in good faith and observe those duties of cooperation,[283] and all persons, whether or not they are parties to the cause, have the duty to collaborate in the discovery of the truth, answering whatever is asked of them, submitting to the necessary inspections, providing whatever is requested and practising the acts that are

275. Articles 352 *et seq.* CC ('confissão').
276. Articles 362 *et seq.* CC ('prova documental').
277. Article 388 CC ('prova pericial').
278. Article 390 CC (prova por inspeção).
279. Article 392 CC ('prova testemunhal').
280. Article 415 CPC.
281. Article 7(1) CPC.
282. Article 7(2) and (3) CPC.
283. Article 8 CPC.

determined.[284] Refusal of due collaboration is sanctioned by fine, and if the refusing person is a party, the court freely assesses the value of the refusal for probative purposes.[285] For instance, the Lisbon Court of Appeal found that 'the reversal of the burden of proof, under Article 344 (2) of the Civil Code and Article 417 (2) of the Civil Procedure Code, presents itself as a civil sanction for violating the principle of cooperation between the parties to discover the material truth […], when this lack of collaboration goes to the point of making it impossible or particularly difficult for the procedural subject burdened with the burden of proof in general terms to produce evidence and is culpable, in the sense that the refusing party could and should act otherwise mode'.[286]

291. Portuguese civil procedure recognizes various types of evidence that parties can use to support their claims or defences, including testimonial evidence, documentary evidence, expert evidence, material evidence, and presumptions of fact. The admissibility of each type of evidence is governed by specific requirements and criteria.

292. Presumption of fact means that, in certain situations, the law may establish a presumption of fact, which can shift the burden of proof to the opposing party. Presumptions are the inferences that the law or the judge draws from a known fact to establish an unknown fact. The beneficiary of a statutory presumption is exempted from the burden of proving the fact.[287] In some cases, statutory presumptions are absolute (*juris et* de jure), i.e., they do not admit proof against them, but in general, presumptions are only relative (*juris tantum*), i.e., it is possible to produce evidence against the presumption.[288] Moreover, court presumptions are only allowed where witness evidence is accepted.[289]

293. Portuguese civil procedure follows the adversarial principle, which means that the parties have the responsibility to present and challenge the evidence. Each party has the opportunity to cross-examine witnesses, challenge the admissibility of evidence and present counter-evidence. Parties have the right to object to the admissibility of evidence presented by the opposing party. Objections can be made based on grounds such as lack of relevance, unlawfulness, or violation of procedural rules. The court will consider these objections and make a ruling on the admissibility of the evidence. To ensure the fairness and reliability of the evidence presented, the judge plays an active role in the examination and evaluation of evidence: he has the authority to ask questions to witnesses, request additional evidence, and the discretion to determine the admissibility of evidence.

284. Article 417(1) CPC.
285. Article 417(2) CPC. Reasons for legitimate refusal include physical or moral integrity of persons, privacy, and professional or State secrecy, according to Article 417(3) CPC.
286. TRL judgment of 18 Sep. 2023, case No. 6249/21.5T8VNG.P1, www.dgsi.pt.
287. Article 349 CC; vd. STJ judgment of 11 Apr. 2019, case No. 8531/14.9T8LSB.L1.S1, www.dgsi .pt.
288. Article 350 of the CC.
289. Article 351 of the CC.

Chapter 3. Administration of Evidence

294. The administration of evidence involves various methods and procedures to obtain and present evidence in court. Aspects regarding the administration of evidence in civil procedure include forced production of documents, deposition by witnesses ('depoimento de testemunhas') and deposition by the parties themselves ('depoimento de parte'), expert evidence ('prova pericial'), inspection by judge ('inspeção judicial'), and affidavit ('declaração').

§1. Forced Production of Documents

295. Documentary evidence is provided by written documents, such as contracts, records, correspondence, or other written materials. In principle, the documents must be presented with the pleading in which the corresponding facts are alleged.[290] However, the opinions of lawyers, professors or technicians can be gathered in the courts of first instance at any stage of the process.[291] Material evidence are physical objects or tangible items that can be presented in court.[292]

296. If a party refuses to produce certain documents that are relevant to the case, the court may order the forced production of those documents, compelling the party or a third party to submit the requested documents. When the opposing party or a third person holds a relevant document, the interested party requires that it be notified to present the document, and the court orders notification, subject to a fine for non-compliance, if it finds that the facts that the party intends to prove are of interest for the decision of the cause.[293]

§2. Deposition by Witnesses and Deposition by the Parties Themselves

297. Witnesses who have relevant knowledge about the case may be called to provide testimony in court. Witness testimony can be obtained through oral depositions during the trial proceedings. Witnesses are questioned by the parties' attorneys, and their testimonies are recorded and considered evidence in the case.

298. Testimonial evidence means testimony provided by witnesses who have direct knowledge or expertise relevant to the case. Any of the parties may request the personal appearance of the opposing party to provide testimony, information or clarification on facts that are of interest to the decision of the case, and the judge may determine it at any stage of the proceedings ('depoimento de parte').[294] The parties may also request, until the beginning of the oral allegations in first instance,

290. Article 423(1) CPC.
291. Article 426 CPC.
292. Article 416 CPC.
293. Articles 429, 430 and 432 CPC.
294. Article 452 CPC.

the provision of declarations on facts in which they have personally intervened or of which they have direct knowledge.[295] Parties to the lawsuit have the opportunity to present their version of the facts and answer questions posed by the opposing party or the court. The testimony of the parties is considered evidence in the case.[296]

299. Concerning the order of testimonials, if both parties have to testify before the court, the defendant testifies first and then the plaintiff.[297] Before testimonial, the court requires the deponent to take the following oath: 'I swear on my honor that I will tell the whole truth and only the truth'.[298] The deposition is always reduced to writing, in the part in which the deponent confesses or in which he narrates facts or circumstances that imply indivisibility of the confessional statement.[299]

300. The capacity to testify as witnesses is recognized by all those who have the mental aptitude to testify about the facts that are the object of the evidence, and it is up to the judge to verify the natural capacity of the persons listed as witnesses, with a view to assessing the admissibility and credibility of the respective testimony.[300] However, those who can testify as parties in the cause are prevented from testifying as witnesses.[301] Moreover, close relatives may refuse to testify as witnesses (and the judge must warn them about that), except in actions, the object of which is to verify the birth or death of children, for example, the ascendants in the causes of the descendants and the adopters in those of the adopted ones, and vice versa, or any of the spouses, or former spouses, in cases to which the other spouse or former spouse is a party.[302]

301. Witnesses testify at the final hearing, in person or via teleconference, except in the cases of: (a) inquiry in advance, (b) inquiry by rogatory letter ('carta rogtória'), (c) inquiry at the residence or at the headquarters of the services, (d) impossibility of appearing in court, (e) inquiry reduced to writing, (f) testimony given in writing, or (g) clarifications provided through the use of the telephone or other means of direct communication between the court and the witness, provided that it is compatible with the nature of the facts to be investigated or clarified.[303]

§3. Expert Evidence

302. Expert evidence involves the presentation of opinions or evaluations provided by experts in specific fields relevant to the case. Experts are appointed by the

295. Article 463 CPC.
296. *See* Article 452 CPC ('depoimento de parte').
297. Article 458 CPC.
298. Article 459(2) CPC.
299. Article 463(1) CPC.
300. Article 495 CPC.
301. Article 496 CPC.
302. Article 497(1) and (2) CPC.
303. Article 500 CPC (referring to the provisions of inquiries of witnesses not taking place at the final hearing).

court or chosen by the parties to provide their professional opinion on technical, scientific, or specialized matters. The expert's report and testimony are considered evidence and can assist the court in understanding complex issues.

303. Expert evidence corresponds to opinions or evaluations provided by experts in specific fields relevant to the case. It can be requested by either party or determined *ex officio* by the judge to an appropriate establishment, laboratory or official service or, when this is not possible or convenient, carried out by a single expert appointed by the judge from among people of recognized suitability and competence in the matter in question.

304. Forensic expertise (medico-legal) is carried out by medico-legal services or by contracted medical experts under the terms set out in the law that establishes the legal regime for carrying out medico-legal and forensic expertise.[304] The party that requested the diligence cannot withdraw from it without the consent of the opposing party.[305]

305. The result of the expertise is expressed in a report, in which the expert or experts give a reasoned opinion on the respective object, which is then notified to the parties for possible revision claims.[306] Where any of the parties does not agree with the expert report, a second expert examination can be ordered by the court upon a well-reasoned request by any of the parties if it finds it necessary for establishing the truth.[307]

§4. Inspection by Judge

306. In certain situations, the judge may conduct an inspection of the relevant place or object related to the case. This allows the judge to directly observe the circumstances and gather evidence. The judge's observations during the inspection are considered evidence in the case.

307. Whenever it deems convenient, the court may, on its own initiative or at the request of the parties, inspect things or persons in order to clarify any fact of interest to the decision of the cause. For this purpose, the court is able to go to the place of the question or to have the facts reconstituted when deemed necessary. However, the court's powers of inspection have to respect the privacy of private and family life and human dignity.[308]

308. The party requesting the inspection by the judge has to provide the court with adequate means to carry it out unless it is exempt or waived from paying costs

304. Enacted by Law No. 45/2004, of 19 August.
305. Article 474 CPC.
306. Articles 484 and 485 CPC.
307. Article 487(1) and (2) CPC.
308. Article 490(1) CPC.

under legal aid rules.[309] A record from the inspection is drawn up in which all the useful elements for the examination and decision of the cause are recorded, and the judge may order that photographs be taken to be attached to the process.[310]

§5. Affidavit

309. Another form of evidence that can be presented to the court is the affidavit. It is a written statement made under oath by a party or a witness. Affidavits are signed and sworn before a notary or a court official, and they contain factual information or statements relevant to the case. For legal purposes, it is considered an authentic document, which proves the facts therein mentioned as done by the concerning authority or public officer, as well as facts therein certified on the basis of perceptions of the issuing entity, but concerning personal judgments of the issuer, their value is left to the discretion of the court,[311] in conditions similar to those of party statement.[312] It is understood that affidavit may have a complementary function to other means of proof, but, as exclusive evidence, it is, in principle, not accepted.

§6. Early Production of Proof

310. If there is a justifiable fear that it will become impossible or very difficult for certain persons to testify or verify certain facts by means of an expert examination or inspection, the testimony, expert examination or inspection may be carried out in advance and even before the filing of the lawsuit.[313] Statements (testimonies, witnesses) given in advance or by letter by the parties are always recorded or, where it is not possible, reduced to writing, with the wording dictated by the judge and the text revised by the parties.[314]

309. Article 490(2) CPC.
310. Article 493 CPC.
311. Article 371(1) of the CC.
312. Article 466 CPC.
313. Article 419 CPC.
314. Article 422 CPC.

Part VIII. Particular Proceedings

311. Several particular proceedings are used to address specific situations or types of disputes, for example, summary proceedings, enforcement proceedings, family and minors proceedings, labour proceedings, insolvency proceedings, and arbitration proceedings.

312. Summary proceedings ('sumário') are a faster and simplified form of civil proceedings used for certain types of cases, such as small claims or cases with clear-cut issues. Summary proceedings aim to expedite the resolution of disputes by reducing procedural formalities and allowing for a more streamlined process. Each particular proceeding in Portuguese civil procedure has its own specific rules, procedures, and requirements. Summary proceedings are used, for example, in executive proceedings for payment of a certain amount based on an arbitration or judicial decision in cases where this should not be executed in the process itself or an application for an injunction to which executive force has been given.[315]

313. Enforcement proceedings ('executivo') are used to enforce court judgments or other enforceable titles, such as authentic instruments or private agreements with executive force. These proceedings involve measures to seize assets, garnish wages, or take other actions to satisfy the debtor's obligation.[316]

314. Family and minors proceedings ('família e menores') deal with matters related to family law, such as divorce, child custody, parental rights, and adoption. These proceedings have specific rules and procedures designed to protect the interests of family members, particularly children.[317]

315. Labour proceedings ('trabalho') pertain to disputes between employers and employees, such as wrongful dismissal, unpaid wages, or workplace discrimination. Labour proceedings have specific rules and procedures aimed mainly at ensuring the protection of employees' rights.[318]

316. Insolvency proceedings ('insolvência') are used when a person or a company is unable to meet its financial obligations and seeks debt relief or bankruptcy

315. Article 550(1) and (2) CPC ('processo sumário para pagamento de quantia certa').
316. Articles 703 *et seq.* CPC.
317. *See* e.g. Articles 989 (alimony) and 994 (divorce) CPC.
318. 'Código de Processo do Trabalho', enacted by Decree-Law No. 480/99 of 9 November.

protection. These proceedings involve the assessment of the debtor's assets, the satisfaction of creditors' claims, and the restructuring or liquidation of the debtor's assets.[319] The purpose of insolvency proceedings is the liquidation of the assets of an insolvent debtor and the distribution of the proceeds obtained by the creditors or the satisfaction of these in the manner provided for in an insolvency plan that, in particular, is based on the recovery of the company included in the insolvency estate. Insolvency proceedings are urgent[320] (e.g., they continue to run on legal holidays) and take precedence over the ordinary work of the court; the judge has only three working days to make a preliminary assessment of the request and also three working days to declare insolvency, when the presentation is made by the debtor.[321]

319. Insolvency Code ('Código da Insolvência e da recuperação de Empresas'), enacted by Decree-Law No. 53/2004 of 18 March, as last amended by Decree-Law No. 57/2022 of 25 August.
320. Article 9 of Insolvency Code.
321. Articles 27 and 28 of Insolvency Code.

Part IX. Conservatory Attachment and Enforcement of Judgments

Chapter 1. Conservatory Attachment ('Penhora Judicial')

§1. Proceedings

317. Conservatory attachment ('penhora'), also known as provisional attachment or provisional measures, is a legal mechanism in Portuguese civil procedure that allows a party to secure or preserve assets or rights pending the resolution of a dispute. It serves to prevent the other party from disposing of or encumbering assets that may be necessary to satisfy a potential judgment.

318. The party seeking conservatory attachment must initiate specific proceedings requesting the attachment. This typically involves filing a motion or a request with the court detailing the grounds for the attachment and providing supporting evidence. The court will review the request and may schedule a hearing to hear arguments from both parties.

319. After the party seeking conservatory attachment files the motion, the court will review the request and consider various factors before granting or denying the attachment. The court will assess the urgency of the situation, the likelihood of success in the main claim, and the potential harm that would result if the attachment is not granted. The court's decision is subject to judicial review and can be appealed by either party.

320. To obtain conservatory attachment, the party seeking it must demonstrate the existence of specific legal grounds and meet certain requirements. The grounds for attachment can vary depending on the nature of the claim but typically involve factors such as the risk of dissipation of assets, the likelihood of non-payment, or the need to secure evidence. The party seeking attachment may be required to provide a guarantee or security deposit to cover any damages that may result from the attachment if it is later determined to be unjustified.

321. Conservatory attachment can take different forms depending on the nature of the assets or rights being preserved. Common types of attachment include the seizure of bank accounts, the seizure of movable assets, the attachment of real estate properties, or the freezing of shares or other financial assets. The specific type of attachment requested will depend on the circumstances of the case.

322. Conservatory attachment applies to all assets of the debtor that can be seized and that, under the terms of the substantive law, are liable for the enforceable debt.[322] Notwithstanding, the attachment applies only to the assets necessary for the payment of the enforced debt and the foreseeable expenses of the execution, which are presumed to amount to 20%, 10% and 5% of the value of the execution, depending on whether it falls within the threshold of the district court (< EUR 5,000), exceeds this threshold and does not exceed four times the threshold of the Court of Appeal (> EUR 5,000 < [4 x EUR 30,000)], or exceeds this latter value (EUR 120,000).[323]

323. However, there is property that is absolutely or totally unseizable, for example, rights the parties cannot dispose of (e.g., personality rights), assets in the public domain of the State, tombs, or pets.[324] Moreover, some property is relatively unseizable, such as, in principle, labour tools and objects that are indispensable for the exercise of the defendant's professional activity or training,[325] and other property is only partially seizable, including two-thirds of the net part of the salaries, wages, periodic benefits paid by way of retirement or any other social benefit, insurance, accident compensation, annuity, or benefits of any kind whatsoever which ensure the subsistence of the defendant.[326]

324. The defendant's property is seized even if it is in the possession of a third party for any reason whatsoever, without prejudice, however, to any rights which the latter may have against the creditor.[327] As for prior diligences, the seizure is carried out after the steps that the enforcement agent considers useful for the identification or location of attachable assets.[328] Where these are not found within three months of the notification, the enforcement agent notifies the debtor and the creditor to specify which assets they wish to be attached to the execution, as well as the creditor to specify which assets he wishes to see seized in the execution, and the defendant is also noticed that the omission or false declaration is subject to a penalty payment.[329] The execution is extinguished without further action, if neither the plaintiff nor the defendant indicates attachable assets within ten days.[330]

325. If there are attachable assets, attachment begins with those which pecuniary value is easier to realize and which are appropriate to the amount of the creditor's claim, and the priority of seizure indicated by the creditor is respected by the

322. Article 735(1) CPC.
323. Article 735(3) CPC.
324. Article 736 CPC.
325. Article 737(2) CPC.
326. Article 738(1) CPC.
327. Article 747(1) CPC.
328. Articler 749(1) CPC.
329. Article 750(1) CPC.
330. Article 750(2) CPC.

enforcement agent, unless for instance it violates a mandatory statutory provision or offends the principle of proportionality of the seizure.[331] In particular, where the property is the permanent home of the defendant, it may only be seized under special (ultima ratio) circumstances.[332] In any case, a defendant who opposes enforcement may, at the time of opposition, request that the attachment be replaced by a suitable security that also guarantees the purposes of enforcement.[333]

§2. Judicial Review

326. In case of seizure of the defendant's assets, he may oppose it on reasons of inadmissibility of the attachment of the goods actually seized or the extent to which it was carried out, or of immediate attachment of assets that are only subsidiarily liable for the debt enforced, or of the attachment affecting property which should not have been affected by the procedure because it is not liable under substantive law for the debt enforced.[334]

327. The defendant may provide security to stay the execution, and if it continues, neither the creditor nor any other creditor may obtain payment without providing security while the opposition is pending. In case it is upheld, the enforcement agent proceeds to the lifting of the seizure and the cancellation of any records.[335] A stay of execution can also be requested by any creditor in order to prevent payments, demonstrating that the recovery of the company or the insolvency of the debtor was necessary.[336]

331. Article 751(1) and (2) CPC.
332. Article 751(4) CPC.
333. Article 751(8) CPC.
334. Article 784(1) CPC.
335. Article 785(3), (4) and (5) CPC.
336. Article 793 CPC.

Chapter 2. Enforcement of Judgments

§1. Enforcement of Domestic Judgments

328. The enforcement of domestic judgments involves the process of executing and enforcing a court judgment or decision within the country. This process ensures that the successful party can obtain the benefits or remedies granted by the judgment.

329. Enforcement proceedings can be for payment of a certain sum,[337] as well as for the delivery of a certain good,[338] or for de facto delivery.[339] Nonetheless, the judgment is only enforceable once it has become final and unappealable, unless the appeal lodged against it has merely 'returning' effect,[340] i.e., it does not stay the execution. Decisions rendered by arbitral tribunals are enforceable in the same manner as decisions rendered by ordinary courts.[341]

I. Proceedings (Executory Attachment and Execution)

330. The enforcement process often begins with an executory attachment ('penhora judicial'), which is a measure used to secure the debtor's assets to satisfy the judgment (*see supra*). The successful party, known as the creditor, can request an executory attachment from the court. The court will issue an order to seize and attach the debtor's assets, such as bank accounts, real estate, or other valuable property. The attached assets can be sold or used to satisfy the creditor's claim.

331. Once the assets are attached, the creditor can proceed with the execution phase to enforce the judgment. The court oversees the execution process, which may involve selling the attached assets through public auction or other means to satisfy the creditor's claim. The proceeds from the sale are used to pay the creditor, and any remaining amounts are returned to the debtor.[342]

II. Judicial Review ('Revisão Judicial')

332. During the enforcement process, both the creditor and the debtor have the right to request a judicial review of the execution proceedings. This allows them to raise objections or challenge the enforcement actions taken by the court. For example, the debtor may argue that the attachment was improperly executed or that

337. Articles 724 *et seq.* CPC ('execução para pagamento de quantia certa').
338. Articles 859 *et seq.* CPC ('execução para entrega de coisa certa').
339. Articles 868 *et seq.* CPC ('execução para prestação de facto').
340. Article 704(1) CPC ('efeito devolutivo').
341. Article 705(2) CPC.
342. Article 811 *et seq.* CPC.

the creditor is seeking an excessive amount. The court will review the objections raised and make a decision on whether to modify or uphold the enforcement measures.

333. If either party is dissatisfied with the court's decision on the judicial review, they may have the right to file an appeal. The appeal process allows the party to present their case before a higher court and seek a review of the lower court's decision. The appellate court will examine the legal arguments and the evidence presented to determine whether the lower court's decision should be affirmed, modified, or reversed.

334. The general rule is that appeals brought against decisions rendered in declaratory proceedings or incidents, which are part of the enforcement proceedings, are governed by the provisions established for appeals ('apelação') in declaratory proceedings.[343] Notwithstanding, there is also a special guarantee of appeal from certain decisions, such as those on determining the suspension, extinction or annulment of enforcement, on the annulment of the sale, and on the exercise of the right of pre-emption or redemption.[344] As for appeals of review ('recurso de revista'), they are limited only to the judgments of the Court of Appeal delivered on appeal in liquidation procedures not dependent on simple arithmetic calculation, verification and grading of claims and in opposition proceedings against enforcement may be reviewed under the general terms, without prejudice to the cases in which an appeal to the STJ is always admissible.[345]

§2. Recognition and Enforcement of Foreign Judgments

335. The recognition and enforcement of foreign judgments involves the process of giving legal effect to a judgment issued by a foreign court within the Portuguese legal system.

I. Rules Applicable in the Absence of a Treaty

336. In the absence of an international treaty governing the recognition and enforcement of foreign judgments, the recognition and enforcement of foreign judgments in Portugal is subject to certain rules. The basic principle is that a decision on private rights rendered by a foreign court is only effective in Portugal, whatever the nationality of the parties, if it is reviewed and confirmed, unless the decision is invoked in proceedings pending before the Portuguese courts as a simple means of evidence subject to the assessment of those who are to judge the case.[346]

343. Article 853(1) CPC.
344. Article 853(2) CPC.
345. Article 854 CPC.
346. Article 978 CPC.

337. Jurisdiction for revision and confirmation of foreign judgments belongs to the Court of Appeal of the territory of the domicile of the defendant.[347] In order for the judgment to be confirmed, certain requirements of the Portuguese legal system have to be met, such as jurisdictional competence of the foreign court, due process, and compatibility with Portuguese public policy. In particular:[348] (a) there can be no doubt as to the authenticity of the document on which the judgment is based or as to the intelligence of the decision; (b) it has acquired the authority of a final decision under the law of the country in which it was given; (c) it comes from a foreign court whose jurisdiction has not been invoked in fraud of the law and which does not deal with a matter falling within the exclusive jurisdiction of the Portuguese courts; (d) the exception of lis pendens or res judicata cannot be invoked on the basis of a case assigned to a Portuguese court, unless it was the foreign court that prevented the jurisdiction; (e) the defendant has been duly summoned to the action, in accordance with the law of the country of the court of origin, and the principles of adversarial proceedings and equality of the parties have been observed in the proceedings; and (f) it does not contain a decision the recognition of which would lead to a result manifestly incompatible with the principles of international public order of the Portuguese State.

338. The recognition and enforcement of a foreign judgment typically require a formal request to be submitted to the competent Portuguese court. The court will review the request and may hold a hearing to examine the judgment's compliance with the necessary requirements. The other party is given notice to contest on those grounds of refusal, and the decision of the Court of Appeal on the merits of the case may be appealed against by review before the STJ.[349]

339. More in detail, submitted with the application is the document that contains the decision to be reviewed, and the other party is notified to contest within fifteen days. The application can only be contested upon grounds of lack of any of the requirements that must be fulfilled for the foreign judgment to be reviewed and upon other grounds of revision provided for in the Code of Civil Procedure. At its own motion, the court checks whether the mandatory requirements are fulfilled and it denies confirmation where any of those requirements is not met, e.g., where proceedings have not observed the principles of contradictory and equality of the parties. The decision of the court can be appealed from the review appeal to the STJ.

II. International Treaties and EU Regulation Brussels I recast

340. Portugal is a party to several international treaties and conventions that govern the recognition and enforcement of foreign judgments. These treaties establish specific rules and procedures for recognizing and enforcing judgments from contracting states.

347. Article 979 CPC.
348. Article 980 CPC.
349. Articles 981 to 985 CPC.

341. To begin with, Portugal is a party to the Hague Convention on the Recognition and Enforcement of Foreign Judgments in Civil and Commercial Matters of 1 February 1971.[350] Moreover, as a member of the EU, Portugal applies the provisions of EU regulations on the recognition and enforcement of judgments issued by other EU Member States, in particular, Regulation Brussels I recast, officially known as Regulation (EU) No. 1215/2012, which governs the recognition and enforcement of foreign judgments within the Member States of the EU.

342. This regulation establishes uniform rules and procedures to facilitate the free circulation of judgments and promote legal certainty within the EU. It applies to civil and commercial matters, covering a wide range of civil and commercial disputes, including contractual claims, tort claims, and matters relating to property rights, and it sets out rules to determine the jurisdiction of courts within the EU, based upon the principles such as the defendant's domicile, the place of performance of an obligation, and the existence of exclusive jurisdictional rules.

343. Under the Regulation Brussels I, a judgment rendered in one EU Member State is automatically recognized in other Member States without any special procedure. This means that a judgment given in one Member State can be enforced in another Member State without the need for a separate recognition process. Despite the general principle of automatic recognition, recognition and enforcement can be refused on the grounds of public policy of the Member State where enforcement is sought, where the defendant was not properly served, or where the judgment is irreconcilable with a judgment given in the Member State where enforcement is sought.

344. The Regulation also includes provisions on the procedures for enforcing foreign judgments. It establishes the principle of 'exequatur', which requires the judgment creditor to obtain a declaration of enforceability from the court of the Member State where enforcement is sought. Once the declaration is granted, the judgment can be enforced as if it were a judgment of that Member State.

345. The principle of mutual trust in the administration of justice in the Union justifies judgments given in a Member State being recognized automatically without the need for any procedure except in cases of dispute and demands the procedure for making enforceable in one Member State a judgment given in another to be efficient and rapid, so that the declaration that a judgment is enforceable is issued virtually and automatically after purely formal checks of the documents supplied, without there being any possibility for the court to raise of its own motion any of the grounds for non-enforcement provided for by this Regulation. Nonetheless, in order to respect the rights of the defence, the defendant is able to appeal in an adversarial procedure, against the declaration of enforceability, if he considers that any of

350. https://www.hcch.net/en/instruments/conventions/full-text/?cid=78.

the grounds for non-enforcement occurs. Redress procedures are also available to the claimant where his application for a declaration of enforceability has been rejected.[351]

346. The Regulation provides a comprehensive notion of *judgment*, according to which 'judgment' means 'any judgment given by a court or tribunal of a Member State, whatever the judgment may be called, including a decree, order, decision or writ of execution, as well as the determination of costs or expenses by an officer of the court'.[352] This notion of 'judgment' seems to include 'foreign interim/ preliminary measures'.[353] Concerning the recognition and enforcement of settlements, the conditions are identical to those provided for authentic instruments and which follow procedures similar to judgments.[354]

347. A judgment given in a Member State is to be automatically recognized in the other Member States without any special procedure.[355] However, recognition is to be denied in case one or more of the following situations occur,[356] such as: (a) recognition is manifestly contrary to *public policy* in the Member State in which recognition is sought;[357] (b) it concerns a judgment given in default of appearance, if the defendant was not served with the document which instituted the proceedings or with an equivalent document in sufficient time and in such a way as to enable him to arrange for his defence (*inaudita altera pars*), unless the defendant failed to commence proceedings to challenge the judgment when it was possible for him to do so; (c) it is irreconcilable with a judgment given in a dispute between the same parties in the Member State in which recognition is sought; (d) it is irreconcilable with an earlier judgment given in another Member State or in a third State involving the same cause of action and between the same parties, provided that the earlier judgment fulfils the conditions necessary for its recognition in the Member State addressed.

348. Moreover, in case recognition is contested by an interested party – either as the principal issue in a dispute or as an incidental question[358] – a judgment is not to

351. Regulation Brussels I recast, recitals 26 to 30.
352. Article 2(a) of Brussels I recast.
353. These are excluded from the notion of judgment provided for in the Hague Convention, which however does not govern such measures according to Articles 4(1) and 7. The European Community has declared, in accordance with Article 30 of the Convention on Choice of Court Agreements that it exercises competence over all the matters governed by this Convention. Member States will not sign, ratify, accept or approve the Convention, but shall be bound by the Convention by virtue of its conclusion by the European Community'.
354. Articles 58(1) and 59 of Brussels I recast.
355. Article 52 of Brussels I recast.
356. Article 45(1), points (a) to (d) of Brussels I recast.
357. *See* CJEU judgment of 11 May 2000, C-38/98, *Régie Nationale des Usines Renault SA v. Maxicar SpA and Orazio Formento* [2000] *ECR* I-2973 ('the decision from a court of a Member State to recognize the existence of an intellectual property right in car body parts, and to confer on the holder of that right protection by enabling him to prevent third party trading in another Member State from manufacturing and commercializing in that State, cannot be considered to be contrary to public policy').
358. Article 36(1) and (2) of Brussels I recast.

be recognized if it was given by a court without jurisdiction, according to Brussels I recast, concerning namely matters relating to insurance, consumer contracts, and proceedings subject to exclusive jurisdiction.[359] In the examination of such grounds of jurisdiction, the court or authority applied is bound by the findings of fact on which the court of the Member State of origin based its jurisdiction.[360] However, this justification for non-recognition of the judgment is not to be raised by the courts of their *own motion* because the jurisdiction of the court of the Member State of origin may not be reviewed and the test of public policy may not be applied to the rules relating to jurisdiction.[361] Moreover, under no circumstances may a foreign judgment be reviewed as to its substance.[362]

349. Concerning *enforcement* in other Member States, the judgment must be declared enforceable in the Member State of origin on the application of any interested party, to be submitted to a specific court or competent authority, which issues the declaration of enforceability 'immediately' on completion of certain formalities and without any review of the impediments of recognition.[363] It means that the courts are not to raise of their own motion the grounds for non-enforcement. Nonetheless, the decision on the application for a declaration of enforceability may be appealed against by either party.[364] A *declaration of enforceability* is to be refused or revoked by the competent Court of Appeal only on one of the grounds that justify non-recognition,[365] but under no circumstances may the foreign judgment be reviewed as to its substance.[366]

350. Settlements are not judgments, as the CJUE ruled in *Emilio Boch*: 'The definition of a "judgment" given in Article 25 of the [Brussels] Convention […] refers, for the purposes of the application of the various provisions of the Convention in which the term is used, solely to judicial decisions actually given by a court or tribunal of a Contracting State deciding on its own authority on the issues between the parties. That is not the case as far as a settlement is concerned, even if it was reached in a court of a Contracting State and brings legal proceedings to an end, because settlements in court are essentially contractual in that their terms depend first and foremost on the parties' intention.'[367]

351. However, a settlement which has been approved by a court in the course of proceedings and is enforceable in the Member State in which it was concluded is to

359. Article 45(1) of Brussels I recast.
360. Article 45(2) of Brussels I recast.
361. Article 45(3) of Brussels I recast.
362. Article 52 of Brussels I recast.
363. Article 41 of Brussels I recast.
364. Article 43(1) of Brussels I recast.
365. Article 45 of Brussels I recast. *See* TRLs, judgment of 16 Dec. 2008, proc. 10053/2008-1, at www.dgsi.pt/.
366. Article 45(1) and (2) of Brussels I recast.
367. Judgment of 2 Jun. 1994, C-414/92, *Solo Kleinmotoren GmbH v. Emilio Boch* [1994] *ECR* I-2237.

be enforced in the State addressed under the same conditions as authentic instruments:[368] the settlement must be declared enforceable in the Member State of origin on the application of any interested party, to be submitted to a specific court or competent authority,[369] which issues the declaration of enforceability 'immediately' on completion of certain formalities and without any review of the impediments of recognition.[370] However, as provided for authentic instruments,[371] in case an appeal is lodged, the competent court can refuse or revoke a declaration of enforceability only in case enforcement of the instrument is manifestly contrary to public policy in the Member State addressed. It means that a declaration of enforceability cannot be refused or revoked upon any other grounds that justify non-recognition.

352. Recognition of judgments and provisional measures handed down after ex parte proceedings is to be denied where it concerns a judgment given in default of appearance, if the defendant was not served with the document which instituted the proceedings or with an equivalent document in sufficient time and in such a way as to enable him to arrange for his defence, unless the defendant failed to commence proceedings to challenge the judgment when it was possible for him to do so[372] (*see supra*). '*Ex parte measures* mean, in the context of provisional measures, temporary orders issued by the court based on one part's request without hearing from the other side.'[373]

368. Article 59, *ex vi* Article 58(1) of Brussels I recast.
369. Articles 38(1) and 39(1) of Brussels I recast.
370. Article 41 of Brussels I recast.
371. Article 58(1), 2nd period, of Brussels I recast.
372. Article 45(1)(b) of Brussels I recast.
373. Green Paper on the Review of Council Regulation (EC) No. 44/2001 on Jurisdiction and the Recognition and Enforcement of Judgments in Civil and Commercial Matters, COM (2009) 175 final, p. 8, fn. 13.

Part X. Out-of-Court Dispute Resolution

353. Out-of-court dispute resolution refers to the methods and processes used to resolve disputes outside of traditional court proceedings. These methods aim to facilitate the resolution of conflicts through negotiation, mediation, arbitration, or other alternative dispute resolution (ADR) mechanisms. Parties involved in a dispute can voluntarily choose to engage in these methods, either before or during court proceedings, to try to resolve their dispute in a more efficient and amicable manner. Out-of-court dispute resolution is encouraged and supported by various legal provisions so that the parties consider out-of-court dispute resolution methods before resorting to formal court proceedings. The specific procedures and requirements for out-of-court dispute resolution in Portugal vary in function of the chosen method and the applicable laws or regulations.

Chapter 1. Arbitration

354. Arbitration proceedings ('arbitragem') are an alternative to court litigation, where parties submit their dispute to an arbitrator or an arbitral tribunal for a binding decision. Arbitration proceedings have their own rules and procedures, which are typically agreed upon by the parties in an arbitration agreement. Arbitration is a form of alternative dispute resolution, which has since 1986 been enshrined in the Portuguese legal system, and it nowadays is governed by the 2011 Arbitration Act.[374]

355. The parties conclude in writing an arbitration convention to submit the decision to arbitrators of their choice, insofar as the dispute is not specifically allocated to a court or to compulsory arbitration and does not concern unavailable rights.[375] The arbitration convention may be either an arbitral compromise ('compromisso arbitral') when it has a current dispute for object – even if it is allocated to a court of law – or an arbitration clause ('cláusula compromissória') when it comprises future disputes resulting from a certain contractual or extra-contractual legal relation.[376]

356. Entities willing to formally promote voluntary arbitration must request the Minister of Justice to establish arbitration centres, taking into account, in particular, the provisions set out in the law.[377] The arbitration centres are entities that, besides providing information, make available to the citizens' mediation and conciliation and if an agreement is not reached through any of these forms, the arbitration is in the form of an Arbitral Tribunal. The arbitration centres function within their own territorial jurisdiction (geographic area), according to the subject matter (type of disputes that they may solve) and, as a rule, according to the value (ceiling set for the disputes). There are several arbitration centres for consumer law and others in the car sector, industrial property, internet domain names, and trade and corporate names.

357. Arbitration is a private and binding form of dispute resolution where the parties agree to submit their dispute to one or more arbitrators, who act as private judges. The arbitrators hear the evidence, consider the arguments, and render a decision, which is called an arbitral award and is binding on the parties. Arbitration is often governed by specific rules and procedures agreed upon by the parties.

358. The Voluntary Arbitration Act provides a legal framework for resolving disputes through arbitration. Key aspects of arbitration include arbitrability of the dispute, arbitration agreement, composition of arbitral tribunal, conduct of arbitral proceedings, arbitral award, appeal from the arbitral award (recurso), and recognition and enforcement of arbitration awards.

---

374. Law No. 63/2011 of 14 December ('Lei da Arbitragem Voluntária').
375. Articles 1 and 2 of Law No. 63/2011.
376. Article 1(3) of Law No. 63/2011.
377. Decree-Law No. 425/86 of 27 December

§1. Arbitrability

359. The principle of arbitrability determines which types of disputes can be resolved through arbitration. In general, civil and commercial disputes are considered arbitrable, meaning they can be submitted to arbitration, including non-property issues, as long as they are allowed under freedom of contract.[378] Certain matters, such as civil rights and liberties, family law, criminal matters, and certain administrative matters, are generally considered non-arbitrable.

§2. Arbitration Agreement and Party Autonomy ('Convenção de Arbitragem')

360. The parties involved in a dispute must have a valid and enforceable arbitration agreement, which is a contract that establishes their consent to submit their dispute to arbitration. The principle of party autonomy allows the parties to determine the procedure and rules that will govern the arbitration, including the choice of arbitrators, the seat of arbitration, and the language of the proceedings. The arbitration agreement must be, expressly or implicitly, in writing and define the object of arbitration or the disputed legal relationship.[379]

§3. Composition of Arbitral Tribunal

361. The arbitral tribunal is composed of one or more arbitrators, who are appointed by the parties or as agreed upon in the arbitration agreement. There can be only one arbitrator or more, and there will be three in case the parties cannot agree on the number of arbitrators, who must be impartial and independent. If the parties cannot agree on the appointment of arbitrators, the court may assist in the appointment process.[380]

§4. Interim Measures and Preliminary Awards

362. The arbitral tribunal has the power to grant interim measures to protect the parties' rights and to preserve the status quo during the arbitration proceedings. These measures can include injunctions, asset freezing, or preservation orders. The tribunal may also issue preliminary awards on specific matters before rendering the final award.[381]

---

378. Article 1(1) and (2) of Arbitration Act.
379. Article 2 of Arbitration Act.
380. Articles 8, 9 and 10 of Arbitration Act.
381. Articles 20 *et seq.* Arbitration Act.

§5. Conduct of Arbitral Proceedings

363. The arbitration proceedings are conducted according to the rules agreed upon by the parties or, in the absence of an agreement, in accordance with the procedural rules set forth in the Arbitration Statute. The proceedings typically involve the submission of written statements, oral hearings, witness testimony, and the presentation of evidence.

§6. Arbitral Award ('Sentença Arbitral')

364. The arbitral award is the final decision rendered by the arbitral tribunal, resolving the dispute between the parties. The award is binding and enforceable upon the parties. It must be in writing, adopted by the majority of arbitrators, and state the reasons for the decision.[382] The general term of the decision is twelve months upon the acceptance of the last arbitrator.[383]

§7. Annulation of the Arbitral Award ('Impugnação')

365. Under Portuguese arbitration law, there are limited grounds for annulling an arbitral award.[384] The parties may only seek to set aside the award before state courts based on specific grounds, for example, a lack of arbitration agreement, breach of due process, or violation of public policy.[385]

366. The state court which annuls the arbitration award cannot decide on the merits of the disputed question or questions, which have to be heard by arbitration courts.[386]

§8. Recognition and Enforcement of Arbitration Awards

367. Arbitral awards, whether domestic or international, can be recognized and enforced in Portugal. The procedure for recognition and enforcement is governed by the Portuguese CPC and the New York Convention on the Recognition and Enforcement of Foreign Arbitral Awards, to which Portugal is a party.[387] Portugal has made the reservation that, within the scope of the principle of reciprocity, Portugal will only apply the Convention in the event that foreign arbitral awards have been handed down in the territory of States bound to it.

---

382. Articles 39, 40 and 42 of Arbitration Act.
383. Article 43(1) Arbitration Act.
384. Article 46 of Arbitration Act.
385. Article 46(3) of Arbitration Act.
386. Article 46(9) of Arbitration Act.
387. https://www.newyorkconvention.org/.

368. In principle, sentences handed down by courts or arbitrators in a foreign country can only serve as a basis for execution after being reviewed and confirmed by the competent Portuguese court, without prejudice to what is established in treaties, conventions, community regulations and special laws.[388]

369. Concerning EU law, arbitration is excluded from the scope of application of Brussels Regulation Brussels I.[389] The preamble of the Regulation reads that 'where a court of a Member State, exercising jurisdiction under this Regulation or under national law, has determined that an arbitration agreement is null and void, inoperative or incapable of being performed, this should not preclude that court's judgment on the substance of the matter from being recognised or, as the case may be, enforced in accordance with this Regulation.

370. This should be without prejudice to the competence of the courts of the Member States to decide on the recognition and enforcement of arbitral awards in accordance with the Convention on the Recognition and Enforcement of Foreign Arbitral Awards, done at New York on 10 June 1958 ('the 1958 New York Convention'), which takes precedence over this Regulation. / This Regulation should not apply to any action or ancillary proceedings relating to, in particular, the establishment of an arbitral tribunal, the powers of arbitrators, the conduct of an arbitration procedure or any other aspects of such a procedure, nor to any action or judgment concerning the annulment, review, appeal, recognition or enforcement of an arbitral award'.[390]

388. Article 706(1) CPC.
389. Article 1(2)(d) of Brussels I recast.
390. Recital 12 of Brussels I recast

Chapter 2. Mediation

§1. Legislation/Definitions

371. Mediation is a facilitated negotiation process where an impartial third party, the mediator, assists the parties in reaching a mutually satisfactory resolution. The mediator helps facilitate communication, identify common interests, and explore possible solutions. Mediation is a confidential process, and the mediator does not make decisions but helps the parties find a mutually acceptable outcome. It is a means of fast alternative dispute resolution.

372. Portugal has a Mediation Statute,[391] which establishes the legal framework for mediation in civil and commercial matters and defines it as a voluntary and confidential process in which a neutral and impartial third party, the mediator, assists the parties in reaching a mutually acceptable solution to their dispute. Concerning EU Law, Directive 2008/52/EC[392] of the European Parliament and of the Council of 21 May 2008 on certain aspects of mediation in civil and commercial matters, which had already been implemented by means of amending the former CPC,[393] defines mediation as 'a structured process, however named or referred to, whereby two or more parties to a dispute attempt by themselves, on a voluntary basis, to reach an agreement on the settlement of their dispute with the assistance of a mediator. This process may be initiated by the parties or suggested or ordered by a court or prescribed by the law of a Member State. / It includes mediation conducted by a judge who is not responsible for any judicial proceedings concerning the dispute in question. It excludes attempts made by the court or the judge seised to settle a dispute in the course of judicial proceedings concerning the dispute in question'.[394]

373. The Portuguese CPC provides that, during court proceedings, the judge, in any state of the cause and whenever deemed convenient, may order the referral of the case for mediation, staying the instance, except when one of the parties expressly opposes such referral.[395] But the initiative to resolve the dispute by mediation can belong to the parties, agreeing to stay the proceedings for a maximum period of three months. If the parties cannot reach an agreement in mediation, the mediator informs the court of this fact, or if an agreement is reached in mediation, it is sent to the court.[396]

391. Enacted by Law No. 29/2013 of 18 April.
392. Directive 2008/52/EC of the European Parliament and of the Council of 21 May 2008 on certain aspects of mediation in civil and commercial matters.
393. Law No. 29/2009 of 29 June.
394. Article 3(a) of Directive 2008/52/EC of the European Parliament and of the Council of 21 May 2008 on certain aspects of mediation in civil and commercial matters.
395. Article 273(1) CPC.
396. Article 273(2), (4) and (5) CPC.

§2. Rights That Can Be Subject to Mediation

374. Mediation can be used to resolve civil and commercial disputes, including matters related to contracts, torts, family law, labour law, and other civil rights. However, certain rights, such as criminal offences and certain administrative matters, including liability of the State for acts and omissions in the exercise of State authority (*acta iure imperii*), are generally excluded from mediation.[397]

§3. Mediation Agreement

375. Mediation requires the parties to sign a mediation agreement, either as a clause of a contract ('convenção de mediação')[398] or, regardless of that, by means of a 'protocolo de mediação' which sets out the terms and conditions of the mediation process.[399] The agreement includes the scope of the dispute, the rights and obligations of the parties, the role of the mediator, and the rules governing the mediation procedure.

§4. Persons/Institutions That Can Act as Mediator

376. The mediator must be impartial, competent and must have completed a recognized training program in mediation. Mediators can be chosen by the parties or appointed by mediation centres or institutions. Mediation carried out in Portugal is subject to several principles, regardless of the entity that carries out the mediation (public or private) or the matter in question, including the necessary requirements for the mediation agreement to have the same value as a court sentence (principle of enforceability) without the need for approval (homologation) by a judge. Among those requirements, there is, in particular, the need for the conflict to be mediated by a mediator who is part of a public mediation system or who is registered on the list of conflict mediators organized by the Ministry of Justice.[400]

§5. Mediation Procedure

377. The mediation procedure involves several stages, which begin with the initial phase, where the mediator explains the mediation process to the parties and obtains their consent to participate. The parties then engage in negotiation and communication facilitated by the mediator, exploring possible solutions to the dispute. The mediator assists the parties in reaching a settlement agreement through active listening, promoting dialogue, and helping them to identify common interests.

397. Articles 10 and 11 of Law No. 29/2013.
398. Article 12 of Law No. 29/2013.
399. Article 16 of Law No. 29/2013.
400. Article 9 of of Law No. 29/2013.

378. Mediation is voluntary and confidential. The content of mediation sessions may not be disclosed or used as evidence in court or any other instance (except in extreme situations where this is essential, namely to defend the best interests of the child or the life or physical integrity of those involved).[401]

§6. SETTLEMENT AGREEMENT

379. If the parties reach a mutually acceptable solution during mediation, they can formalize their agreement in a settlement agreement. The settlement agreement is a legally binding document that outlines the terms and conditions of the settlement reached. Once signed by the parties, the settlement agreement has the same effect as a court judgment and can be enforced accordingly.[402]

380. In a mediation process, the disputing parties are responsible for the decisions they make with the help of the mediator, who, unlike a judge or arbitrator, has no decision-making power. In fact, the mediator does not impose any deliberation or sentence, as he only guides the parties, helping them to establish (or re-establish) the necessary communication so that they can find, by themselves, the basis of the agreement that will put an end to the conflict. The content of the agreement is freely fixed by the parties and must be reduced to writing, signed by the parties and by the mediator.[403] In cases of coercion, fraud, mistake, or if the agreement is contrary to public policy, the parties can request the court to set aside the settlement agreement.

§7. INTERNATIONAL MEDIATION

381. International mediation – i.e., mediation conducted across national borders – can be governed by international treaties, such as the Singapore Mediation Convention, by the parties' agreement on the applicable rules and procedures.

401. Article 5(4) of Law No. 29/2013.
402. Article 9 of Law No. 29/2013.
403. Article 20 of Law No. 29/2013.

Chapter 3. Other Types of Out-of-Court Dispute Resolution, Such as Collaborative Lawyering

382. 'Collaborative lawyering', as an alternative form of dispute resolution that aims to settle conflicts through a cooperative and non-adversarial approach, is not specifically regulated.

383. However, it may be an option for out-of-court dispute resolution, as lawyers in Portugal have duties towards the community. They are obliged to defend rights, freedoms and guarantees, to fight for the proper application of laws, for the prompt administration of justice and for the improvement of culture and legal institutions, and in special, they have an obligation to collaborate in access to the law.[404] As a way to collaborate in access to the law, 'collaborative lawyering' may be a legitimate out-of-court method to solve disputes.

384. Collaborative law involves the parties and their respective attorneys working voluntarily together to reach a mutually beneficial settlement to resolve the dispute outside of court. The parties and their lawyers sign a collaborative participation agreement establishing the framework for the process and the principles and guidelines that will govern the negotiations, emphasizing open communication, transparency, and the commitment to finding a mutually satisfactory resolution.

385. The parties' attorneys act as facilitators and problem-solvers rather than adversarial advocates, assisting clients in identifying and addressing their interests, managing emotions, and exploring creative options for settlement, possibly involving other professionals, such as financial experts or mental health professionals, if their expertise is relevant to the dispute. In collaborative lawyering, the emphasis is on finding solutions that meet the interests of all parties involved rather than focusing solely on legal rights or positions. Confidentiality is key to encouraging open and frank discussions without the fear that statements made during the process will be used against the parties later.

386. Collaborative lawyering does not yet have a relevant role as an alternative dispute resolution mechanism like arbitration and mediation. However, it may be an effective method for resolving disputes in a cooperative and amicable manner, without prejudice to other means of dispute resolution, provided that mandatory rules or rights the parties cannot dispose of are not at stake.

404. Article 90(1) and (2)(f) of Statute of the Bar Association.

Selected Bibliography

AA, VV. *O Novo Processo Civil: Contributos da Doutrina para a Compreensão do Novo Código de Processo Civil.* Lisboa: Centro de Estudos Judiciários, 2013 (*The New Civil Procedure: Contributions of the Doctrine to the Understanding of the New Code of Civil Procedure*).

Almedina, Francisco Manuel Ferreira de. *Direito Processual Civil* – vol. 1. 3.ª ed. Coimbra: Almedina, 2022 (*Civil Procedural Law*).

Almedina, Francisco Manuel Ferreira de. *Direito processual civil* – vol. 2. 3.ª ed. Coimbra: Almedina, 2019 (*Civil Procedural Law*).

Andrade, Manuel A. *Domingues de. Noções Elementares de Processo Civil.* Coimbra: Coimbra Editora, 1956 (*Elementary Notions of Civil Procedure*).

Barrocas, Manuel Pereira. *Lei de Arbitragem Comentada.* 2.ª ed. Almedina: Coimbra, 2018 (*Commented Arbitration Law*).

Barrocas, Manuel Pereira. *Manual de Arbitragem.* 2.ª ed. Almedina: Coimbra, 2013 (*Arbitration Handbook*).

Botelho, João. *Processo Civil.* Braga: Nova Causa, 2021 (*Civil Procedure*).

Cordeiro, António Menezes. *Tratado da Arbitragem.* Almedina: Coimbra, 2016 (*Treaty on Arbitration*).

Cura, António A. *Vieira. Curso de Organização Judiciária.* 2.ª ed. Coimbra: Coimbra Editora, 2014 (*Judicial Organization Course*).

Cura, António A. *Vieira. Organização Judiciária Portuguesa.* Coimbra: Gestlegal, 2018 (*Portuguese Judicial Organization*).

Freitas, José Lebre de. *A Ação Executiva – À luz do Código de Processo Civil de 2013.* 7.ª ed. Coimbra: Gestlegal, 2017 (*The Executive Action – In Light of the 2013 Code of Civil Procedure*).

Freitas, José Lebre de. *Código de Processo Civil Anotado* – vol. 1. 4.ª ed. Coimbra: Almedina, 2018 (*Annotated Code of Civil Procedure*).

Freitas, José Lebre de. *Código de Processo Civil Anotado* – vol. 2. 4.ª ed. Coimbra: Almedina, 2019 (*Annotated Code of Civil Procedure*).

Freitas, José Lebre de. *Código de Processo Civil Anotado* – vol. 3. Coimbra: Almedina, 2022 (*Annotated Code of Civil Procedure*).

Freitas, José Lebre de. *Estudos sobre Direito Civil e Processo Civil.* 2ª ed. Coimbra: Coimbra Editora, 2009 (*Studies on Civil Law and Civil Procedure*).

Freitas, José Lebre de. *Introdução ao Processo Civil – Conceito e Princípios Gerais à luz do Novo Código.* 4.ª ed. Coimbra: Gestlegal, 2017 (*Introduction to Civil Procedure – Concept and General Principles in light of the New Code*).

Selected Bibliography

Freitas, José Lebre de. *Novos Estudos sobre Direito Civil e Processo Civil.* Coimbra: Gestlegal, 2021 (*New Studies on Civil Law and Civil Procedure).*

Freitas, José Lebre de. *O Processo Civil na Constituição.* Coimbra: Coimbra Editora, 2008 (*Civil Procedure in the Constitution*).

Geraldes, António Abrantes, Pimenta Paulo & Sousa Luís Filipe de. *Código de Processo Civil Anotado* – 2 vols 2.ª ed. Coimbra: Almedina, 2022 (*Annotated Code of Civil Procedure*).

Geraldes, António Santos Abrantes. *Recursos em Processo Civil.* 7.ª ed. Coimbra: Almedina, 2022 (*Appeals in Civil Procedure*).

Geraldes, António Santos Abrantes. *Temas da Reforma do Processo Civil* – vol. IV. 4.ª ed. Coimbra: Almedina, 2010 (*Topics of Civil Procedure Reform*).

Gonçalves, Marco Carvalho. *Lições de Processo Civil Executivo.* 5.ª ed. Coimbra: Almedina, 2022 (*Lessons on Executive Civil Procedure*).

Gouveia, Mariana França. *Curso de Resolução Alternativa de Litígios.* 3.ª ed. Almedina: Coimbra, 2014 (*Alternative Dispute Resolution Course*).

Machado, António Montalvão & Pimenta Paulo. *O Novo Processo Civil.* 12.ª ed. Almedina: Coimbra, 2010 (*The New Civil Procedure*).

Marques, J.P. *Remédio. Acção Declarativa à Luz do Código Revisto.* 3.ª ed. Coimbra: Coimbra Editora, 2011 (*Declarative Action in the Light of the Revised Code*).

Marques, J.P. Remédio. *Direito Processual Civil da Propriedade Industrial.* Almedina: Coimbra, 2022 (*Civil Procedure Law of Industrial Property*).

Martins, Alexandre de Soveral. *Um Curso de Direito da Insolvência* – vol. I, 4.ª ed. Almedina: Coimbra, 2022 (*A Course in Insolvency Law*).

Mendes, João de Castro & Sousa Miguel Teixeira de. *Manual de Processo Civil* – 2 vols. Lisboa: AAFDL, 2023 (*Civil Procedure Handbook*).

Mesquita, Miguel. Apreensão de *Bens em Processo Executivo e Oposição de Terceiro.* 2.ª ed. Coimbra: Almedina, 2001 (*Seizure of Assets in Executive Proceedings and Third Party Opposition*).

Mesquita, Miguel. *Reconvenção e Excepção no Processo Civil.* Almedina: Coimbra, 2009 (*Counterclaim and Exception in Civil Procedure*).

Monteiro, António Pedro Pinto, Silva Artur Flamínio da & Mirante Daniela. *Manual de Arbitragem.* Almedina: Coimbra, 2019 (*Arbitration Handbook*).

Oliveira, Elsa Dias. *Arbitragem Voluntária: Uma Introdução.* Almedina: Coimbra, 2020 (*Voluntary Arbitration: An Introduction*).

Pimenta, Paulo. *Processo Civil Declarativo.* 3.ª ed. Coimbra: Almedina, 2023 (*Declarative Civil Procedure*).

Pinto, Rui Gonçalves. *A Ação Executiva.* Lisboa: AAFDL, 2023 (*The Executive Action*).

Ramos, José Luís Bonifácio. *Estudos de Direito Civil e de Direito Processual Civil.* Lisboa: AAFDL, 2021 (*Studies on Civil Law and Civil Procedure Law).*

Ribeiro, Virgínio da Costa & Rebelo Sérgio. *A Ação Executiva Anotada e Comentada.* 3.ª ed. Coimbra: Almedina, 2021 (*The Executive Action: Annotated and Commented*).

Rodrigues, Fernando Pereira. *Noções Fundamentais de Processo Civil.* 2.ª ed. Coimbra: Almedina, 2019 (*Fundamental Notions of Civil Procedure*).

Rodrigues, Fernando Pereira. *O Novo Processo Civil – Os Princípios Estruturantes*. Almedina: Coimbra, 2013 (*The New Civil Process – The Structuring Principles*).

Rodrigues, Fernando Pereira. *Os meios de prova em processo civil*. 3.ª ed. Almedina: Coimbra, 2017 (*Evidence in Civil Proceedings*).

Santos, Hugo Luz dos. *Direito Civil e Direito Processual Civil Contemporâneo: Entre a Dogmática e a Prática*. Braga: Nova Causa, 2021 (*Civil Law and Contemporary Civil Procedural Law: Between Dogmatics and Practice*).

Silva, Paula Costa e. *Perturbações no cumprimento dos negócios processuais*. Lisboa: AAFDUL, 2020 (*Disturbances in the Fulfillment of Procedural Negotiations*).

Silva, Paula Costa e. *Acto e Processo: Regressando ao dogma da irrelevância da vontade na interpretação e nos vícios do acto postulativo*. Thomson Reuters, Revista dos Tribunais, 2019 (*Act and Process: Returning to the Dogma of the Irrelevance of the Will in the Interpretation and Defects of the Postulative Act*)

Silva, Paula Costa e. *Estudos de Arbitragem*. 3 vols. Almedina: Coimbra, 2022 (*Arbitration Studies*).

Silva, Paula Costa e. *Responsabilidade por Conduta Processual – Litigância de Má Fé e Tipos Especiais*. Almedina: Coimbra, 2022 (*Liability for Procedural Conduct – Bad Faith Litigation and Special Types*).

Silva, Paula Costa e, Lourenoço Paula Meira & Henriques Sofia. *Direito Processual Civil I e II* – vol. I. Elementos de trabalho (Programa, Casos Práticos, Testes e Exames), Lisboa: AAFDUL, 2012 (*Civil Procedure Law I and II*).

Silva, Paula Costa e & Reis Nuno Trigo dos. *A prova ilícita*. Lisboa: AAFDUL 2019 (*The illicit Evidence*).

Sousa, Miguel Teixeira de. *Introdução ao Processo Civil*. Lex: Lisboa, 2000 (*Introduction to Civil Procedure*).

Varela, João de Matos Antunes & Nora J. Miguel Bezerra e Sampaio e. *Manual do Processo Civil*. 2.ª ed. Coimbra: Coimbra Editora. 1985 (*Civil Procedure Handbook*).

Vicente, Dário Moura. *Lei da Arbitragem Voluntária Anotada*. 6.ª ed. Almedina: Coimbra, 2023 (*Annotated Voluntary Arbitration Law*).

Legislation: https://diariodarepublica.pt/dr/home.

Court judgments: http://www.dgsi.pt/.

https://e-justice.europa.eu/.

Legislation

Administrative and Tax Courts Statute, enacted by Law No. 13/2002 of 19 February ('Estatuto dos Tribunais Administrativos e Fiscais').

Administrative Procedure Code, enacted by Decree-Law No. 4/2015 of 7 January ('Código de Procedimento Administrativo').

Arbitration Act, enacted by Law No. 63/2011 of 14 December ('Lei da Arbitragem Voluntária').

Association Statute, enacted by Law No. 145/2015 of 8 September (Estatuto da Ordem dos Advogados).

Brussels Convention on Jurisdiction and the Enforcement of Judgments in Civil and Commercial Matters, concluded on 27 September 1968, and Lugano Convention on Jurisdiction and the Enforcement of Judgments in Civil and Commercial Matters, concluded on 16 September 1988 between Member States and EFTA States (revised in 2007).

Civil Code, enacted by Decree-Law No. 47344 of 25 November 196 ('Código Civil').

Civil Procedure Code, enacted by Law No. 41/2013 of 26 June ('Código de Processo Civil').

Code of Civil Registry, enacted by Decree-Law No. 131/95 of 6 June ('Código do Registo Civil').

Commercial Registration Code, enacted by Decree-Law No. 403/86 of 3 December ('Código do Registo Comercial').

Consumer Act, enacted by Law No. 24/96 of 31 July ('Lei de defesa do consumidor').

Copyright and Related Rights Code, enacted by Decree-Law No. 63/85 of 14 March (as last amended by Decree-Law No. 47/2023 of de 19 June).

Council Directive No. 2003/8/EC, of 27 January, on improving access to justice in cross-border disputes through the establishment of common minimum rules regarding legal aid in the context of such disputes.

Criminal Procedure Code, enacted by Decree-Law No. 78/87 of 17 February ('Código de Processo Penal').

Directive (EU) 2020/1828 of the European Parliament and of the Council of 25 November 2020 on representative actions for the protection of the collective interests of consumers and repealing Directive 2009/22/EC.

Directive 2004/48/EC of the European Parliament and of the Council, of 29 April 2004 on the enforcement of intellectual property rights.

Directive 2008/52/EC of the European Parliament and of the Council of 21 May 2008 on certain aspects of mediation in civil and commercial matters.

Directive 2013/11/EU of the European Parliament and of the Council of 21 May 2013 on the alternative resolution of consumer disputes.

Industrial Property Code, enacted by Decree-Law No. 110/2018 of 10 December ('Código da Propriedade Industrial').

Insolvency Act, enacted by Decree-Law No. 53/2004 of 18 March ('Código da Insolvência e da Recuperação de Empresas').

Judges Statutes, enacted by Law No. 21/85 of 30 July ('Estatuto dos Magistrados Judiciais').

Judicial System Organization Statute, enacted by Law No. 62/2013 of 26 August (Lei da Organização do Sistema Judiciário' – LOSJ).

Judiciary Police Statute, enacted by Decree-Law No. 14/2010 of 15 November ('Polícia Judiciária').

Justice of Peace Statute, enacted by Law No. 78/2001, of 13 July ('Julgados de Paz').

Labour Procedure Code, enacted by Decree-Law No. 480/99 of 9 November ('Código de Processo do Trabalho').

Labour Procedure Code, enacted by Decree-Law No. 480/99 of 9 November ('Código de Processo do Trabalho').

Lawyers' Acts Statute, enacted by Law No. 49/2004 of 24 August ('Lei dos Atos Próprios dos Advogados').

Legal Costs Regulation, enacted by Decree-Law No. 34/2008, of 26 February, as last amended by Law No. 9/2022 of 11 January ('Custas Judiciais').
Mediation Act, enacted by Law No. 29/2009 of 29 June ('Lei da Mediação').
Notarial Code, enacted by Decree-Law No. 207/95 of 14 August ('Código do Notariado').
of Court Clerks Statute, enacted by Decree-law No. 343/99 of 26 August ('Estatuto dos Oficiais de Justiça').
Ombudsman Statute, enacted by Law No. 9/91 of 9 April ('Estatuto do Provedor de Justiça').
Propular Action Law, enacted by Law No. 83/95 of 31 August ('direito de participação procedimental e de acção popular').
Public Prosecutor Statute, enacted by Law No. 68/2019 of 27 August (Estatuto do Ministério Público')
Real Estate Registry Code, enacted by Decree-Law No. 224/84 of 6 July ('Código do Registo Predial').
Regulation (EU) No. 1215/2012 of the European Parliament and of the Council of 12 December 2012 on jurisdiction and the recognition and enforcement of judgments in civil and commercial matters.
Solicitors and Bailifs Statute, enacted by Law No. 154/2015 of 14 September ('Estatuto da Ordem dos Solicitadores e dos Agentes de Execução').
The Hague Convention of 30 June 2005 on Choice of Court Agreements.

Selected Bibliography

Index

The numbers here refer to paragraph numbers.

Index

www.ingramcontent.com/pod-product-compliance
Lightning Source LLC
Chambersburg PA
CBHW071351230926
51846CB00002B/516